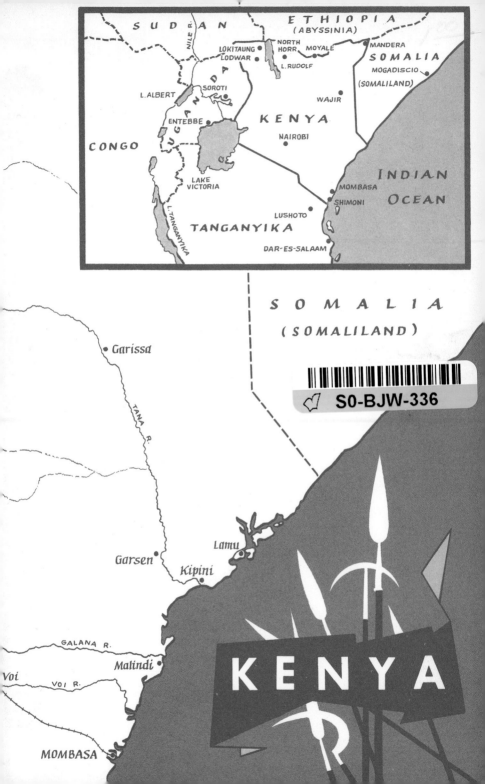

SUDAN
ETHIOPIA
(ABYSSINIA)
NORTH
HORR
MOYALE
MANDERA
LOKITAUNG
LODWAR
SOMALIA
L. RUDOLF
MOGADISCIO
(SOMALILAND)
L. ALBERT
SOROTI
WAJIR
ENTEBBE
KENYA
NAIROBI
LAKE
VICTORIA
MOMBASA
SHIMONI
INDIAN
OCEAN
CONGO
LUSHOTO
TANGANYIKA
DAR-ES-SALAAM

SOMALIA
(SOMALILAND)

Garissa

TANA R.

Garsen
Lamu
Kipini

GALANA R.

Voi
Malindi

VOI R.

KENYA

MOMBASA

JOMO KENYATTA:

TOWARDS TRUTH ABOUT "THE LIGHT OF KENYA"

JOMO KENYATTA:

TOWARDS TRUTH ABOUT

"THE LIGHT OF KENYA"

BY GEORGE DELF

DOUBLEDAY & COMPANY, INC., GARDEN CITY, NEW YORK
1961

IN MEMORY OF MERLE,
AND TO ALL THOSE WHO LIVE IN KENYA

INTRODUCTION

LEADING nationalist politicians often acquire contradictory reputations, but few have attracted such controversy as the Kenya African leader, Jomo Kenyatta. Convicted in 1953 of managing the Mau Mau rebellion, which was eventually surpressed at a cost of more than thirteen thousand lives and 50 million pounds, Kenyatta was sentenced to seven years' imprisonment, to be followed by indefinite restriction in some remote area. As late as mid-1960 the Governor of Kenya refused repeated African requests for his release, on the grounds that he was "the African leader to darkness and death" and was a menace to security. The official report on Mau Mau, published at the same time, claimed that Jomo Kenyatta had deliberately misled his followers for his own perverted ends and had "preached a calculated hymn of hate" against his white rulers. And yet, far from diminishing, Kenyatta's popularity among Kenya Africans continued to grow until he became something of a myth.

Kenyatta became in the eyes of his followers a symbol, not of perverted witchcraft and hate, but of African freedom and self-respect. They did not ignore the fact that it was Jomo Kenyatta who had first demanded those political and civil liberties which the British Government had conceded so rapidly, after Mau Mau had revealed the depth of African unrest. At the time of writing, at the end of 1960,

7

it seems that mounting African political pressure will quite soon force the hand of the Kenya Government and secure Kenyatta's release. If and when this happens he may soon become Chief Minister in a Government which has hitherto considered him in the blackest light. Such an event, if present attitudes are not modified, could lead to another crisis in race relations. It has become more important than ever that the events which have led up to this difficult situation should be understood in their true perspective.

There are some people who still think that the bitter quarrels of the past should be forgotten and that all that matters now is that the future should be faced in a spirit of co-operation. It would be pleasant if this could happen, but I do not believe that the mark of so many years can be wished away so lightly. Despite its superficial air of gaiety Kenya has not been an easy place to live in for any of the racial groups here. Conflicting cultures, fear, ignorance, and superstition have all combined to obstruct racial harmony. Whether they are material or psychological, these are real obstacles, and they can only be removed by a determined effort to understand their origins and development. Perhaps all political and social problems are best understood in terms of a human being, and no one has been more closely affected by colonial rule in Kenya than Jomo Kenyatta.

Kenyatta's actions after his release will have repercussions far beyond the borders of Kenya. His actions will undoubtedly owe much to his wide experience in Europe as well as in Kenya of the ways of the white man and Western civilization. The "civilizing mission," which began with such a flourish at the turn of the century, has suffered many defeats as well as victories. Africa will soon prove to have been more than a passive recipient of Western ideas and techniques. When the passions of colonial politics have died down Europe may discover that Africa has taught her some facts about herself which she had never been fully aware of.

In this book I have tried to trace Kenyatta's varied career, which took him from a traditional tribal background to left-wing political circles in England, back to postwar Kenya and desperate attempts to win political rights for his people, and thence to Mau Mau and imprisonment. I think it is worth while, though far from easy, for non-Africans to try to understand how an African saw the efforts of the missionaries, settlers, and administrators to re-create in Africa the way of life which they had learnt in England. As well as the schools and the roads and the hospitals they brought with them their own deep-seated psychological tensions, which had many strange effects on the African people with whom they came into contact, effects which they all too readily attributed to some intrinsic defect in the African mind and his ways. An understanding of Kenyatta's life has its own particular interest, but it may also have good results politically if he returns to power.

While I was compiling this book, Jomo Kenyatta was still under Government restriction in the far-off village of Lodwar, and I was not allowed to visit him there. However, thanks to the generous co-operation of his daughter, Margaret, and of the many other of his friends and relatives, I have been able to find much information which helps to fill in the details of his life. My thanks are also due to many others of all races, some of them very busy people, who have spared their time to discuss with me what they knew of Kenyatta. I am particularly grateful to Elizabeth Kenrick and Jonathan Silvey in London, who spent many hours collecting information concerning Kenyatta's long stay in Europe. Perhaps appropriately, this book was written in the Limuru district of the White Highlands, an area which has long been the focus of political argument in Kenya. This was due to the generosity of the St. Julians' Community, who allowed me the use of their beautiful house. Opinions expressed in the book are of course my own, and are not in any way the responsibility of those whom I have mentioned above. In conclusion I would hope that this book may contribute in a small way towards the essential task of creating a Kenya where race is of no account.

Limuru. 7
December 1960

CHAPTER ONE

WHEN THE WHITE MEN CAME

On his passport at the time of his trial in 1952 the date of birth of Jomo Kenyatta was given as 1893, but, as he said then, this was only an approximate date. The West's preoccupation with hours, minutes, and years had not at that time penetrated East Africa to any great extent, although the Kikuyu tribe to which Kenyatta belonged had already had their first encounter with the "red strangers." For some years tribal prophets had foretold the arrival from distant lands of a powerful people with strange clothes and dangerous weapons, who would bring with them an "iron snake breathing fire and smoke." These first historic meetings may not have been marked with quite the wonder which they deserved but they set the scene for one of the most prolonged dramas of human relations which the world has seen. One of the chief stage-props for this drama, the "iron snake," did indeed follow closely on the heels of the visitors, to be named, prosaically, the Uganda Railway — and to be renamed, even more prosaically, when it later expanded, East African Railways and Harbours. Like a gazelle caught in the headlight of one of the new locomotives, East Africa watched Western civilization move in.

It is difficult, perhaps impossible, for a non-African to do more than guess at what it felt like to live as a member of the Kikuyu tribe at that time. Childish jungle films and authors with a taste for horror have given strangers to

Africa a doubly difficult task if they wish to separate the men and women from the "dancing savages." However, the outlines of Kikuyu tribal life have been well documented so that it is possible to know something of the society in which Jomo Kenyatta spent his early years.

"They looked up at heaven and could see it was far away, sloping gradually down until it rested upon some hills or mountains, and to them that was the end of the world. As to their mode of government, they managed their affairs on a tribal basis. Each tribe had its chiefs or its councils of elders, and its seers and diviners to conduct the affairs of peace and war." This is how Jomo Kenyatta briefly described the old world of the Kenya tribes in a pamphlet written in 1945 called *Kenya, Land of Conflict*. In an age which has tried to move beyond the trite judgments of Victorian morality, it is useless to describe the Kikuyu life of that time as evil and fear-ridden. The modern cold war's "balance of terror" has a solid enough foundation of fear itself. But it is certain that Kikuyu life was culturally restricted and all but static, and the difficulties which have beset the tribe since the beginning of the century have been due far less to an attempt to hang on to old customs than to a fervent desire to accept whole the new ideas to which they were introduced.

At the turn of the century, the Kikuyu tribe was the most numerous in the land that became known to the new white rulers as Kenya. It seems that the word Kenya is the result of a rather faltering attempt to pronounce the Kikuyu name for Mount Kenya, Kere-Nyaga. It is estimated that at that time there were about three quarters of a million Kikuyu, living in an elongated area of land more than a hundred miles long and between twenty and fifty miles wide. At one end, to the northeast, the equatorial snows of Mount Kenya shone serenely high above the scattered fields and huts, and at the other end the Kikuyu cultivation ended at a forest belt, which served as a barrier between these short stocky Bantu agriculturalists and the tall elegant Masai, nomadic herdsmen who had drifted southwards over the centuries from the Nile valley. The Kikuyu land lay at between five and eight thousand feet. The soil was rich and red, the grass and the trees a dark and vivid green. The rain came regularly, in reasonable quantities, sweeping in low from the distant Indian Ocean, three hundred miles away across the plains to the east. At night in the plains the lions stretched and yawned and awoke, as their ancestors had done for centuries. The skulking hyenas moved among the silent beehive huts and the giria sang away the dark hours. The sleeping men and women dreamed — some dreams of contentment and some anxious dreams of hostile spirits.

As the sun rose and burnt through the mists a buzz of human activity spread along the ridges and valleys. Huts were cleaned, crops tended, cattle and goats led to pasture. Ironsmiths made their spears — either to be traded for cattle with the Masai or used on them. If it was a day of ceremonial or ritual, the dances and the feasting followed. If it was a day of fighting, the young men armed and put on their war paint and fought. If it was a day of disaster, the seers came forward and made their ritual preparations. The world of man began at the forest edge and ended at the foot of Kere-Nyaga. All the rest belonged to the arbitrary spirit world and only specially gifted men could glimpse behind its dark curtains. The unquesting embryonic life of Africa moved on quietly and rhythmically.

According to the anthropologists, the Kikuyu tribe originated about six or seven hundred years ago, and their remote ancestors are thought to have migrated from the coastal regions to the east. As the tribe grew it began to take over the neighbouring areas of forest land, thus displacing a small group of prehistoric people, the Agumba, who hunted in the forests and lived in underground dwellings. Towards the end of the sixteenth century a part of the tribe began to move southwards across the Chania River into what is now called the Kiambu district, bordering on a swampy piece of land at the edge of the plains where the "iron snake" was to rest on its journey to Lake Victoria. This halt, prompted by the need for a supply depot, decided the site of what was to grow into the colourful mixture of concrete, bougainvillæa, and politicians that is modern Nairobi.

The tribe was still expanding slowly when two events combined to upset the basic rhythm. The first Europeans began to pass by with their long winding caravans, their strange manners and weapons, and their desire to trade for food. Almost as if disturbed by the impending clash of human cultures, nature let loose a series of devastating assaults in a final effort to retain her age-old dominance of the Kikuyu people. Smallpox cut a swathe of death through the tribe. Rinderpest killed much of the highly valued livestock. The rain did not come and the resultant famine further reduced the tribe. Finally there came a fluttering armada of locusts, which ate their way through such crops as were left. As in the days of the Old Testament, these events created a paralysing impression of divine fury. The best and wisest of the tribe's seers had proved helpless to avert these catastrophes. The ritual sacrifices to the god Ngai (or Mogai), high on the snows of Kere-Nyaga, had had no effect. Terrified, the tribal spirit contracted, driven back by a sense of guilt and failure. The fields, only recently won from the forests, reverted to bush. The "natural fire within the dark wood of life," as Dante described the inner springs of human nature, was burning very low.

It is difficult for those who know that man can now create more havoc than nature to appreciate the effect of natural disaster on a simple people. A brief sketch of Kikuyu tribal patterns may help to explain it. In an anthropological study of his tribe, *Facing Mount Kenya,* written in London in the late thirties, Jomo Kenyatta gives his own account of the tribal origins:

According to the tribal legend, we are told that in the beginning of things, when mankind started to populate the earth, the man Gikuyu, the founder of the tribe, was called by the Mogai (the Divider of the Universe), and was given as his share the land with ravines, the rivers, the forests, the game and all the gifts that the Lord of Nature (Mogai) bestowed on mankind. At the same time Mogai made a big mountain which he called Kere-Nyaga (Mount Kenya), as his resting-place when on inspection tour, and as a sign of his wonders. He then took the man Gikuyu to the top of the mountain of mystery, and showed him the beauty of the country that Mogai had given him. While still on the top of the mountain, the Mogai pointed out to the Gikuyu a spot full of fig trees (*mikoyo*), right in the centre of the country. After the Mogai had shown the Gikuyu the panorama of the wonderful land he had been given, he commanded him to descend and establish his homestead on the selected place which he named Mokorwe wa Gathanga. Before they parted, Mogai told Gikuyu that, whenever he was in need, he should make a sacrifice and raise his hands towards Kere-Nyaga (the mountain of mystery), and the Lord of Nature will come to his assistance.

Gikuyu did as he was told and when he arrived at the fig trees he found waiting for him a beautiful woman named Muumbi (the creator). They had nine daughters but no sons, and when Gikuyu complained to Mogai about this he was told to make a sacrifice of one lamb and one kid beneath the largest fig tree and all would be well. Gikuyu did this, and later when he returned to the tree nine handsome young men were waiting there. They were allowed to marry the nine girls on condition that they accepted the matriarchal system. Their nine families developed over the years into the nine main clans into which the tribe is divided.

The women, however, are said to have abused their special rights and bullied the men unmercifully, till at length the men could stand it no longer, and planned to overthrow their tormentors and rule themselves. This they did in a distinctly ungentlemanly manner, by all making love to the women on one night. Six months later nature had ensured that the women were in no condition to defend their position, and the men accomplished a bloodless revolution. A psychologist might well wonder today, as he observes the firmly subordinate treatment meted out to most Kikuyu women by their menfolk, whether there is not an element of guilty hindsight in this legend.

The god of all things, Ngai, was just one essential part of the complex of Kikuyu religion which Dr. Leakey has described as "the interweaving of three distinct religious concepts which sometimes overlap and sometimes are interlocked."[1] Ngai was supreme. He lived on the mountain tops, but was also to be found everywhere. He had many of the attributes of the Old Testament God, and was almost as dictatorial as the nature he controlled. He could be worshipped either by individuals or groups. In every territorial grouping there was one particular fig tree which

[1] *Mau Mau and the Kikuyu*, L. S. B. Leakey, Methuen, p. 39.

served as a holy place for communal worship. Ngai was not only asked for help in times of disaster but was offered prayers of thanksgiving for such blessings as a good harvest or rainfall.

Ancestral spirits formed the second important religious concept. When the individual died his spirit joined with those of his ancestors. Apart from this there was a kind of communal family spirit which was ever present and which entered into a new member of the family at the sacred rite of "the second birth" during childhood. Prayers to God were always accompanied by prayers to the ancestral spirits of those concerned. Whenever food and drink were prepared some was set aside for the departed members of the family. During the religious ceremony of marriage not only the living members of the two families but the ancestral spirits too were united. Many minor personal and family disasters were interpreted not as the will of Ngai so much as the result of displeasure shown by the ancestors. Dr. Leakey suggests[2] that the third category of religious belief, in spirits which were neither human nor concerned with Ngai, was probably the oldest, though having less significance than the others. This animism centred on particularly prominent natural objects such as waterfalls, large rocks, and trees. When trees were cut down, for example, some were left standing so that the tree spirits would not be deprived of a home.

Often indistinguishable from these manifestations of religious belief was the belief in magic, white and black. Jomo Kenyatta wrote in the Preface to *Facing Mount Kenya:*

As for magic, I have witnessed the performance of magic rites many times in my own home and elsewhere.
    [2] *Ibid.,* p. 43.

My grandfather was a seer and a magician, and in travelling about with him and carrying his bag of equipment I
served a kind of apprenticeship in the principles of the
art. Besides this, I have lived in a place called Gaturi in
Central Kikuyu, a district well-known for its magical prac-
tices, and there came into contact with many magicians or
witch doctors, and learnt a great deal about their ways. I
have also had opportunities of meeting and discussing the
subject with other magicians, both from coastal and up-
country tribes.

Jomo Kenyatta's grandfather was a practitioner of white
magic, known as a *mundo mugu*. His was an important
position because he acted as a kind of visionary, doctor,
and general adviser, as well as magician. He told those
within his influence when the time was ripe for marriage,
for battle, and for other important occasions. Sometimes he
would be approached to supply magic in connection with
any of a number of personal matters, amongst which were
loving, healing, and purifying. Kenyatta says that love
magic, with its recitations and spells, is practiced in some
form or another "by almost every tribe in East Africa," and
he adds, hopefully: "The writer is happy to say that he
had the privilege of trying one of the spells, and it undoubtedly proved successful."[3] That these workers in white
magic were far removed from the typical witch doctors of
the European imagination, whose only object is death and
destruction, is borne out by Dr. Leakey's opinion that they
"held a very honoured place in the tribe, and membership
of the guild was confined to persons who had served a long
apprenticeship before finally being accepted to this calling. Moreover, a man who wished to stand for the profession had to satisfy the other members of the guild that he
had a special 'calling' for such work before he could even

[3] *Facing Mount Kenya*, p. 289.

become an apprentice or trainee. These medicine men were always of outstanding ability and great wisdom. . . ."[4] Had the white man stayed in Europe for a few more years it is quite possible that Jomo Kenyatta would have completed his "apprenticeship" and passed his life in this fashion.

There were, of course, no prisons or lunatic asylums in Kikuyuland and many of the corrupt or mentally unstable Kikuyu seem to have fallen within the sphere of the black magician, or *murogi*. Whereas the *mundu mugo* performed his business in daylight, and never worked against the social unity of the tribe, the practitioner of black magic used superstition for his own ends, to poison and to kill. He was greatly feared, and when caught was often burned to death after an elaborate trial and ceremony. Kenyatta describes how his grandfather took part as a leading elder in "many of these unhappy events." The complex checks and balances of this society ensured that in normal times the destructive side of the Kikuyu nature, exploited by the *murogi*, was repressed, or at worst kept within reasonable limits. There seems little doubt that the failure of the Europeans to differentiate between what was positive and what was destructive in the religious beliefs of the Kikuyu has done much harm. Somewhat acidly Jomo Kenyatta has described some effects of this failure.

Nowadays, even though a *murogi* be really an undesirable or dangerous character, he has no fear of this punishment. For the white man's administration does not usually differentiate between a purely medical and a ceremonial doctor (magician) and the nefarious practitioner, *murogi*, but all go under the name of "witch doctors." All "doctors" and "seers" of every type, even men who can do nothing

4 *Mau Mau and the Kikuyu*, L. S. B. Leakey, p. 47.

but good, are liable to prosecution. Indeed, it is now the innocent who suffer. My grandfather was a "seer," *morathi* or "wise man," whose duty it was to give general advice and foretell the future as far as he could, especially in connection with the war expeditions. He bequeathed his profession, together with his calabashes which were his insignia, to my father, who, however, did not practice, since there were no tribal wars to be conducted.

But missionaries, aided by Government officials, searched the homesteads for the "works of the devil." My father's calabashes were taken as evidence of guilt, and he, with many others in the same position, served a period of imprisonment. . . . It was simply the policy that everything to do with "magic" was to be stamped out, for the missionaries to get rid of "Satan's" influence, and to clear the ground for their proselytising work.[5]

Religion, then, inextricably entwined with magic, played a vital part in the life of the Kikuyu. Without it life meant nothing at all. Neither atheism nor agnosticism could play any part. The other aspects of tribal life formed an equally unquestionable pattern. The family was the basic and most important unit, but it was not a family in the European sense but something far larger. Each family belonged to one of the nine clans, within which were sub-clans, and blood relationships were of great importance, however remote. Some of the early missionaries were horrified at what they took to be an extravagant indulgence in polygamy, but which was in fact merely a strong emphasis on family ties. A man might refer to many women as his wives when in reality he only had one or two, the rest being relatives. Marriage itself was not the callous family bargain it is sometimes supposed to have been. A young man looked around for a girl at one of the tribal dances and if he met

[5] *Facing Mount Kenya*, p. 305.

someone who won his heart he had to win her consent. If and when this happened, the respective families discussed the matter and it was they who decided how much in the way of bride-price should be paid to the parents of the girl. The prevalence of love potions is proof enough that the girls often had very definite ideas of their own as to whom they would be willing to marry.

Politically the Kikuyu had developed a simple but remarkably democratic form of self-government. The average Kikuyu man was especially close, not only to his numerous relatives but also to those of his own age grade. As he grew older he passed through the initiation ceremonies into manhood and became a warrior and a husband. Later he became an elder and, depending on his seniority and his strength of character, he became a member of a council of elders, which in turn owed allegiance of a loose kind to a council of senior elders which represented the local ridge. Kikuyuland is physically marked by many narrow ridges and valleys. Sometimes an exceptionally gifted leader would dominate these councils, but on the whole the spokesman of a council was no more than that, and chiefs did not exist as they did in many other African tribes. The geography of the country, broken up as it was into hills and valleys, may have discouraged the growth of strong central rule and favoured the growth of argumentative individualism for which the Kikuyu are well known.

Lastly, in this brief attempt to portray the kind of life which the Kikuyu were leading when Jomo Kenyatta was born, and when the white man was beginning to make his presence felt, there is the vital matter of land. There was no system of outright individual ownership in the modern European sense, and writing on this point Kenyatta himself says: "It is no more true to say that the land is collectively owned by the tribe than that it is privately owned by the individual. In relation to the tribe a man is the owner of his land, and there is no official and no committee with authority to deprive him of it or to levy a tax on his produce. But in so far as there are other people of his own flesh and blood who depend on that land for their daily bread, he is not the owner, but a partner, or at the most a trustee for the others."[6]

As the Kikuyu expanded towards what is now Nairobi, they bought land from the Dorobo tribe, and it is this land which has been the centre of Kenya's land controversy. By careful and elaborate religious ceremonies the Kikuyu elder would link his ancestral spirits with those of the Dorobo family from whom he was buying the land, usually an area of forest. When the deal had been completed the Kikuyu would move in with his family and establish a sub-clan of his own. Sometimes he would permit some of his less fortunate tribesmen to come and acquire cultivation rights on the new land until such time as he and his family wanted to use it for themselves. The first travellers through this area remarked on the close cultivation, but after the natural disasters which hit the Kikuyu at this time many surviving families retired to their old homes, and large areas of land quickly reverted to bush. Ownership, however, had not been relinquished, and what is equally important is that land could not be sold to anyone outside the sub-clan without the permission of the clan elders. When the first European missionaries and administrators saw this apparently vacant land they not unnaturally assumed, according to their customs, that the land belonged to no one. The alienation of some of this land for use by English settlers caused a shock which echoed through

[6] *Ibid*, p. 311.

every part of the Kikuyu mind and has not yet died away.

From this short survey the reader may catch a glimpse into the life from which Jomo Kenyatta and the Kikuyu people have emerged during this century. "Land," writes Kenyatta, "is the key to the people's life; it secures for them that peaceful tillage of the soil which supplies their material needs and enables them to perform their magic and traditional ceremonies in undisturbed serenity, facing Mount Kenya."[7] These words were written amid the fogs of London in 1937, and distance, coupled with a burning anger at the superior way in which most Europeans had dismissed African life as "primitive savagery," probably accounts for the claim to serenity. The life of the Kikuyu was certainly not the horrible senseless thing imagined by many outsiders even today. It was an extremely elaborate and carefully balanced means of preserving a tolerable life in face of the arbitrary dictatorship of nature. Within the strict and unalterable limits imposed by custom and superstition, life was worth living. The Kikuyu knew very well how to laugh before the European came. But there is little room for serenity when disease and famine can advance at will and break down the fragile defences of the mind and body. Serenity was probably about as scarce in Kikuyuland as it was in London or New York.

It is important to remember that individualism, though clearly latent in the Kikuyu mentality, was kept on a very short rein by both custom and the spirit world. "According to Gikuyu ways of thinking," writes Kenyatta, "nobody is an isolated individual. Or rather, his uniqueness is a secondary fact about him: first and foremost he is several people's relative and several people's contemporary. His life is founded on this fact spiritually and economically,

[7] *Ibid.*, Preface, XXI.

just as much as biologically; the work he does every day
is determined by it, and it is the basis of his sense of moral
responsibility and social obligation. His personal needs,
physical and psychological, are satisfied incidentally while
he plays his part as member of a family group, and cannot
be fully satisfied in any other way." Kikuyu life was rigidly
limited but it was a coherent whole, and it offered to every
man and woman who obeyed the rules a life of adult
responsibility. Under the influence of the more sophisti-
cated ideas of Europe the tight social structure began to
give way, and, after one last tragic attempt to rally, to
crumble into a dying ruin and a memory. The story of
Jomo Kenyatta's life until the present time is as intimately
linked with the desperate attempt of the Kikuyu people to
find a new security within the twentieth-century world as
it is with the quality of that world itself. It is a fascinating
and enigmatic story, strewn with lost opportunities, and
laughter has sometimes appeared as the one thing which
could be salvaged from the muddle. One of the first English settlers in the country, the irrepressible Colonel Ewart
Grogan, now eighty-three and enjoying a fulminating old
age, told me recently: "Of course, the whole thing has been
a complete pantomime from beginning to end." And so it
has, but Kenya's Prince Charming has not always been a
perfect gentleman, the Sleeping Beauty has had a definite
and complicated mind of her own, and the cardboard
swords have sometimes been real.

CHAPTER TWO

THE GREAT HUSH

As THE old man's voice droned on I stared at him and wondered whether he would die peacefully when his turn came, or whether the events of his life had been too confusing for that. We were seated around a small wood fire near three beehive-shaped Kikuyu huts on the crest of one of those ridges which cut across the tribe's reserve in more or less parallel lines. I had driven out from Nairobi, twenty miles or so away, to meet Jomo Kenyatta's brother, and with me were two Kikuyu journalist friends, Henry and Dominic. Henry had a lively wit and used it impartially on nationalists, settlers, and anyone who came within his gaze. Dominic had studied law in London, and at moments when he was not engaged in editing a strongly pronationalist Swahili weekly, he was passionately engaged in coaxing as much coffee out of his unfortunate coffee trees as human ingenuity and natural fertility would allow. The paper was a side line, but not the coffee.

Kenyatta's brother, James Muigai, a handsome man who looked about forty and said he was far more, was away in the nearby village at a co-operative society meeting, but his daughter said that his father (Kenyatta's stepfather), was living up on the hill close by. We walked up past the banana trees and small fields, and Dominic pointed out the place where Jomo Kenyatta used to live before his arrest in 1952. The stone house, he said, had been demolished on Government orders and the stones and material used to build a Red Cross centre in the village. The land had been taken over for the use of a small coffee research station.

We found the old man seated near the fire on a low wooden stool, chatting with a friend. Henry explained why we had come and I was introduced. We sat on the grass and Henry put a series of questions to the old man in Kikuyu while I listened. It was a cool morning, with a matte-grey sky, and a breeze stirred the embers in the fire. Hens pecked jerkily at the stubble nearby, and across the valley came the indistinct noises of a village.

The old man clutched a blanket closer to his dark worn skin, and he stared without expression at the fire as he spoke. His face was marked with many lines and had an air of strength about it. His flat husky voice compared oddly with the eager and slightly amused manner of Henry's questioning. Kenyatta's stepfather was probably a full-grown young warrior before he saw a European and his mind had been formed in the pattern of the old Africa. He would never be initiated into the new ways.

"Jomo was lonely at home," he said, "he was a clever boy, playful and ambitious. Sometimes he stole food from the stores, but it was difficult for the mothers to discover it. He even used to spend whole nights in the bush if he was angry or slighted. He liked handiwork and was good at it. At the age of about ten Jomo ran away. He left a herd of cattle in the field and I was upset about it. He went off to school. After schooling he brought me 190 shillings, a blanket and a piece of linen, and we became reconciled. . . . Afterwards he went off to live at Dagoretti near Nairobi and I did not see much more of him."

The old man finished speaking. I asked Henry to ask him

whether he thought Jomo Kenyatta had led the Mau Mau movement. The response was immediate. "*Aca! Aca!* [No! No!]" he said angrily, and spat in the fire. Would he like Kenyatta to return home? "He is a famous warrior and only such a man can calm the people," he said. We shook hands and left, and the two old men stayed on by the fire.

Change in Kenya has been so rapid that it is sometimes a shock to realise that its entire modern history is still within living memory. At the time when the old man was in his prime, and when Jomo Kenyatta was restlessly tending the cattle, the foundations of Kenya-European thought were being laid. Europe, and England in particular, was brimming over with aggressive self-confidence, and it is not surprising that those who left her shores took away with them their fair share of it, whether they left to trade, to conquer, to govern, or to instruct in the message of Jesus Christ.

The small island in the grey North Sea had sent the waves of her influence to the farthest corners of the world. The "green and pleasant land" was humming with energy and spirited, if rather thoughtless, nationalism. Most Englishmen saw more truth than humour in Gilbert's teasing refrain, "For he himself has said it, and it's greatly to his credit, that he is an Englishman." Large areas of the world had quite casually come under the Union Jack, and thanks to the competitive instinct, which was beginning to dominate Europe's political thinking, it became clear to anyone with an ounce of political sense that if his country did not quickly stake a claim in the newly explored Dark Continent of Africa then somebody else's would. During the last twenty years of the nineteenth century lines had been neatly drawn across the map of Africa and the appropriate colours duly filled in to denote ownership. It was to take about sixty years for Europe to find out what she had done and for Africa to regain consciousness.

There were of course plenty of good motives behind the influx of explorers, missionaries, administrators, and settlers, but the mocking mind of an Irishman thought there was more to the innocent aims of the Englishman than appeared at first sight. George Bernard Shaw used Napoleon in his *Man of Destiny* to spill the moral beans. "No Englishman is too low to have scruples: No Englishman is high enough to be free from their tyranny. But every Englishman is born with a certain miraculous power that makes him master of the world. When he wants a thing he never tells himself that he wants it. He waits patiently until there comes into his mind, no one knows how, a burning conviction that it is his moral and religious duty to conquer those who have got the thing he wants. Then he becomes irresistible. Like the aristocrat he does what pleases him and grabs what he covets: like the shopkeeper he pursues his purpose with the industry and steadfastness that comes from strong religious conviction and deep sense of moral responsibility. He is never at a loss for an effective moral attitude." Hard words, but Shaw knew personally what the English could be like, from experience of their rule in Ireland.

A Scottish geologist, Joseph Thomson, after passing by Kikuyuland in 1883, commented on the Kikuyu: "Murderous and thievish . . . with an utter inability to resist stealing, or the fun of planting a poisoned arrow in the traders." A military engineer engaged on the survey of the Uganda Railway in 1891 thought they were "very excitable, treacherous, and addicted to drink . . . Since Europeans settled in Kikuyu the tribesmen seem to consider that a little war against the fort is a fitting termination to the harvest carnival."

However, a rich Hungarian, Count Teleki, who passed through Kikuyuland in 1887 with an expedition, had rather different views. He found them "shy and timid," despite the "countless tales" he had heard of the "fierceness and hostility of the natives." He wrote of the "charming landscape," and added, "as far as the eye could reach stretched well-cultivated, undulating pasture lands, which were a revelation to us." He went on to describe the appearance of the Kikuyu. "The lively, restless temperament of the Kikuyu is far more indicative of their relations to the great Bantu stock than their physical appearance, which resembles that of the Masai. Though seldom above a medium height they are well built, muscular, and strong. Their characters vary much." The Count thoughtfully observed that the tribe was "destined to play an important part in the future of East Africa."

Another man who recognized some of the better qualities of the Kikuyu was that unashamed and dynamic little imperialist, Lugard, later to be raised to the peerage for his exploits in empire-building.

A cynical young lecturer in Imperial History at Cambridge recently told his somewhat startled audience that Lord Lugard's passionate devotion to the cause of Empire was fundamentally due to an unsuccessful love affair in his youth. This Freudian swipe at the already tottering philosophy of imperialism cannot detract from Lugard's undoubted genius as an organizer and leader. His opinion of the Kikuyu was that they were "a fine, intelligent-looking race . . . I was more favourably impressed by them than any tribe I had as yet met in Africa." Lugard ascribed the rapid change of attitude of the Kikuyu from friendliness

to hostility, to the "want of discipline in the passing caravans, whose men robbed the crops and otherwise made
themselves troublesome; the people became estranged, and
presently murdered several porters." He thought that a
"man of tact and decision could have ruled with little display of force," and concluded: "Africa needs the right men
— men of decision and of character and individuality.
When such men are in charge, you will rarely hear of
bloodshed, of murders, and 'reprisals.' . . ."

Unfortunately the "right men" were rare birds. Robert
Hall, an early administrator after whom the Kikuyu district
of Fort Hall is named, thought his charges "exceedingly
intractable . . . cunning, distrustful, and treacherous . . .
accustomed to look upon all strangers as enemies" — hardly
an auspicious approach to the art of administration. Lord
Cranworth, one of the aristocrats of England who sought
the life of a gentleman settler in Kenya, wrote of the Kikuyu: "An unattractive tribe, riddled with superstition of the
most primitive and repulsive kind." As early as 1900 a man
who was destined to pass through Kenya history with the
noisy insistence of an exploding firecracker was writing:
"There is a sound maxim in the progress of the world, to
the effect that what cannot be utilized must be eliminated.
And drivel as we will for a while, the time will come when
the negro must bow to this as the inevitable . . . Why, because he is black and is supposed to possess a soul, we
should consider him, on account of that combination, ex-
empt, is difficult to understand, when a little firmness
would transform him from a useless and dangerous brute
into a source of benefit to the country and of satisfaction
to himself."[1] The writer was Ewart Grogan, the man who

[1] *From the Cape to Cairo,* Ewart S. Grogan and Arthur H. Sharp,
pp. 350–63.

had recently walked from the Cape to Cairo in order to win a wife and who, in 1960, was still humorously and irascibly enjoying life in Nairobi.

He told me with great glee how, during his prodigious journey a local chief in the Congo had offered him a smoked man as a gift — "completely kippered, my dear chap." Ewart Grogan does not believe in soft-pedalling, and his outspokenness has sometimes caused embarrassment to all sides. At a time when careful "moral attitudes" were being built up to justify the alienation of land in Kenya for the use of settlers he wrote that there was no need for "mawkish euphemisms" to disguise "European land-grabbing schemes" — phrases which probably caused a disconcerted hush in Whitehall. What was needed, said Grogan, was a "good sound system of compulsory labour."

After the more disinterested observations of the explorers had come the practical opinions of the settlers — men of great energy and initiative, in whom almost everything was subordinated to the competitive urge to develop and harness the raw material of nature, including human nature. Even more than the missionaries and the public school-trained administrators, they were representative of a Western civilization which was already suffering from the effects of, in the phrase of the Psalmist, "going a-whoring with its own inventions." An increasing proportion of England's population was leading a drab and poverty-stricken existence in blackened factory towns, a deforming of the human spirit which had already led to a reaction in the formulation of the ideologies of Communism and Socialism.

But high above the grime of factory life lived the small group of men who, by luck, birth, or ruthless energy, had become the managers of this new world. They believed

that success was the reward of God and failure the curse
of the Devil. Even organized Christianity, with exceptions,
drew up its skirts from the dirty streets and prayed for the
status quo. This was the society which sent out its men and
women to Kenya and Africa — some to expend their phe-
nomenal energy and inventive power on taming the land,
and others to take the message of Christ to the "poor
heathen," a message which was either largely ignored or
else cleverly manipulated back in England. Ewart Grogan's
belief in the god of utility was no more than a blunt expression of the urge which inspired his most socially successful countrymen.

The centre of colonization in Kenya — Nairobi — was
still in its infant corrugated-iron stage when the ten-year-
old Jomo Kenyatta wandered into the Church of Scotland
mission station in the village of Kikuyu, about twenty
miles away on the edge of the great Rift Valley. His name
at that time was Kamau, son of Ngengi, and he explained
that he was an orphan from the Fort Hall district. He was
suffering from a spinal disease and was operated on by the
late Dr. J. W. Arthur, who probably saved his life. The
young Kamau was then employed, according to a Scottish
minister now in Nairobi, as a kitchen help by a Mr. J.
Cooke, who nicknamed him "John Chinaman," not altogether on account of his rather slanting eyes. Mr. Cooke
said later of him: "Even at that time he had a great imagination and could spin yarns like an old Chinaman."

Kamau was then accepted by the mission school, which
at that time mixed a more formal education with vocational
training, and he was drafted into the carpentry section.
After a few years of this he was duly baptized and assumed
the Christian name of Johnstone, being now called Johnstone Kamau. He was not considered by his teachers an

outstanding pupil and did not achieve a very high grading. It may be that he found the kind but alien Scottish discipline an irksome curb on his emotional and imaginative nature and he ran away to Nairobi, then, as now, the mecca of all young Kenya Africans with any education. There he was once more helped by his former employer, Mr. Cooke, who worked for the Public Works Department, and he was found a job as a clerk. This act of friendship had a sequel many years later in Liverpool. Jomo Kenyatta, at that time a voluntarily exiled left-wing politician, called on his former benefactor, who, according to an acquaintance, was "in difficult circumstances," and looked after him.

Nairobi was Jomo Kenyatta's first experience of a town run on modern European lines, and every feature of it, from its laws to its buildings and its citizens, must have been a strange new experience for him. At that time, at the beginning of the century, it had all the improvised simplicity of an American frontier town. One of Kenya's first settlers, a young man from the sooty English industrial town of Leeds, reached Nairobi a few years before Jomo Kenyatta. His own surprise at what he found was based on different grounds.

There was no complaint about the view or the acceptability of the climate [he wrote]; to the south and east there were unending grass plains dotted with every kind of antelope. To the north, beyond more grass plains, forests of varying hues. Many of the trees bore sweet-smelling lavender-coloured blossoms. To the west was the rising hill country of the Kikuyu highlands, and the Ngong hills.

I am in slight error. To the south the landscape was interrupted by two huge corrugated-iron buildings; one was the railway shed, the other the railway workshops. Leading from the station in a northerly direction was a wide track known as Station Street, which was eventually to be called Government Road. About four hundred yards from the start of the street there were a number of corrugated-iron houses on its left. They were the residential quarters of the railway employees.

To the right, running parallel with the main track, were nine corrugated-iron buildings, flatteringly called stores or shops. The first one was double-storey and some humorist called it a hotel. This was Victoria Street. On the hill, to the west, a number of corrugated houses could be seen, with young eucalyptus trees sprouting about them. These were the houses of the higher officials.

As Bagnall and I stood in this wilderness of grass we were speechless; then the funny side of it made us laugh. We had come to settle near a town and intended to supply it with the usual things a town requires but it seemed our first job would be to build the town.[2]

This was not the last time laughter was the saving grace of a Kenya situation.

Victoria Street, Station Street, and Government Road — symbolic reminders of the holy trinity of Imperial Britain. Their presence was to be found in every continent of the world. A heavy morality kept guard over the spirit of England, with the solemn pomposity of a public school headmaster frowning over his sixth form, and the little Queen was the keeper of the nation's conscience.

As is common, the local paper was a pretty accurate reflection of life around it. It was published in the old seaport of Mombasa — a steamy little town with strong traces of both Arab and Portuguese influence, and with uncomfortably recent memories of the vicious slave trade, which, over the centuries, is thought to have accounted for upwards of twelve million East Africans. One issue of 1901 carried a brave little poem which needs no comment:

[2] *African Rainbow*, H. K. Binks, pp. 42–43.

Undepressed by seeming failure,
Unelated by success;
Heights attained, revealing higher,
Onward, upward, ever press.

The same issue included a letter complaining of Kikuyu lawlessness and said that the tribe was in a "very unsettled state" and had no respect for authority. An editorial comment entitled "Killed in the Name of God" told how religion was impeding business and preventing the followers of Islam from eating tinned meat. "Could not our butchers be taught to use God's name," wrote the crafty editor, "and a guarantee to that effect be printed on the tins and thus meet the religious scruples of such a great host of His Majesty's subjects?" It was reported that tennis and cricket were well established, and that the main courtroom leaked, thus putting judicial dignity at the mercy of every deluge. The law, in fact, was apparently not always all that it should have been and earned an admonishing editorial: "God help and pity the land when the poor tremble and shrink from its law courts lest they should not get justice."

Colonial pomp and circumstance had begun already to rear its gilded head, and one settler complained about the "petty civilians strutting about the town with gold collars, enormous gold epaulettes and toy swords." The future rift between settlers and officials had begun. An article on administration demonstrated clearly what at least one settler thought of the future. "If we wish to do anything with East Africa we must improve internal and external communication, we must knock every atom of fight out of the natives." A tea planter who had lived in Assam offered readers the fruit of his experience. "The missionaries would only change good coolies into bad ones, and introduce an element of discord. Immediately he turns Christian he is useless as a garden coolie and is only of service as a dummy to hang European clothes on."

A Russian visitor wrote a letter to the paper complaining of the behaviour of Europeans in shops and offices and accused some of being "quite drunk." If they had tried to treat the local people like that in the Russian Asiatic Protectorates, he said, "the reward would be nothing less than the boot." Behaviour in nearby Zanzibar was also not all it could have been and must have caused Britannia a blush or two. "It is not freedom," wrote one observer, "that has filled Zanzibar and Mombasa with harlotry, it is the fruits of slavery. The Head of the State drives through his Capital with forty to fifty concubines in open carriages behind him, lances and flags in front and a Christian cook in the rear. One official is trying to emulate this display of animalism and keeps a harem of six on ten rupees a head." Drink was yet another of the hundred and one unfortunate facts of East African life which prevented the much-talked of "white man's burden" from ever really leaving the ground. Periodic mentions of "yet another officer ruined" testify to the effect of alcohol. Idealism had to be very firm to stand the many difficulties in the way of establishing a Western way of life in East Africa, and perhaps it is surprising that any of it at all was left over for the "great civilizing mission."

The pages of this lively little paper set a pattern for English journalism in Kenya which was to be radically altered only in 1960. The problems, successes, and failures of the European community were fully aired and reported. The African viewpoint was then, and has been almost ever since, virtually ignored, with disastrous results to the level of understanding between the two races. On the whole, the settlers looked upon the African community as a "source of labour" or as a "native problem." There was not the imagination to appreciate the overwhelming fact that three million people were reacting every day of the year to the ways of the new rulers, and drawing their own conclusions. One disastrous conclusion, which in later years spread like a weed in an untended field among many Kikuyu, held that the Bible had been brought to keep the people quiet while their land was being stolen behind their backs. A tragic belief like this highlights what has narrowly escaped being a total breakdown in simple public relations between governing and governed. The fruits of this egocentricity became visible later in the stunned surprise with which many Europeans in Kenya have greeted the sudden emergence of an unchallengeable African political voice.

One visitor to Kenya in those early years made some shrewd comments on its probable future. His name was Winston Churchill. At the time of his visit there were in Nairobi about five hundred Europeans, three thousand Asians, and ten thousand Africans. "Every white man in Nairobi is a politician," he wrote, "and most of them are leaders of parties. . . . There are in miniature all the elements of keen political and racial discord, all the materials for hot and acrimonious debate. The white man versus the black; the Indian versus both; the settler against the planter; the town contrasted with the country; the official class against the unofficial."[3] Even then the problem of colour was becoming serious. "Colour," he wrote, "is already the dominant question at Nairobi. . . . 'We mean to make East Africa a white man's country,' cries, in strident tones, the Colonists' Association on every occasion."[4]

[3] *My African Journey,* Winston Spencer Churchill.

[4] *Ibid.,* p. 45.

Churchill saw too the seeds of potential violence that were being sown amid these conflicting interests. "Behind — very close behind," he wrote, "lie the appeals to force, by mobs or Empires, to decide in a brutal fashion the brutal question which of two sets of irreconcilable interests shall prevail."[5] He warned against the dangers of abandoning the Africans to the "fierce self-interest of the small white population." He recognized, too, the shaky foundation of admiration upon which black acknowledgement of white authority was based. "It would destroy the respect of the native for the white man," he wrote, "if he saw what miserable people we have got at home," and added that civilization was shy of the black man, and was embarrassed "lest he should see what lies behind the gold and purple robe of State, and begin to suspect that the all-powerful white man is a fraud."

Winston Churchill's impressions reflect very well the dilemma of the British encounter with Africa. He was a child of his restless age, and believed that no man had the right to live an idle life. But his urge towards material progress at almost any cost contained an element of genuine doubt. "To compare the life and lot of the African aboriginal," he wrote, "secure in his abyss of contented degradation, rich in that he lacks everything and wants nothing — with the long nightmare of worry and privation, of dirt and gloom and squalor, lit alone by gleams of torturing knowledge and tantalizing hope, which constitutes the lives of so many poor people in England and Scotland, is to feel the ground tremble underfoot . . . in truth the problems of East Africa are the problems of the world. We see the social, racial, and economic stresses which rack modern society already at work here, but in miniature."[6]

[5] *Ibid.*, p. 51.   [6] *Ibid.*

But there was a positive side to Kenya's forcible annexation to the strains and stresses of Europe, and Churchill saw this too. "It was pleasant to hear," he wrote, "with what comprehension and sympathy the officers of the East African Protectorate speak about their work; and how they regard themselves as the guardians of native interests and native rights against those who only care about exploiting the country and its people."[7] Paternalist they may have been, but the members of the Colonial Civil Service in Kenya did in fact stand as a buffer between acquisitive settlers and credulous Africans. It was easy to be paternalist when admiration for the white man had a trusting and childlike quality. This honeymoon of trust is described in another passage from Churchill's account: "So peaceful are the tribes — now that their inter-tribal fighting has been stopped — that white officers ride freely about among their villages without even carrying a pistol. All the natives met with on the road were armed with sword and spear, and all offered us their customary salutations, while many came up smiling and holding out long, moist, delicate-looking hands for me to shake, till I had quite enough of it."[8]

But it is not through the eyes of an acute politician that the mysterious reaches of the African mind can be approached, as it surveyed the coming of the white man. It was left to a settler's wife, a Countess from Denmark, Karen von Blixen, to make this journey of the imagination. In her beautifully drawn book of memoirs, *Out of Africa,* she describes the fascination and the remoteness of African traditional life as she saw it — most of her contacts being with the Kikuyu people on the border of the Masai land. Her ideas may help to complete this attempt to understand

[7] *Ibid.*   [8] *Ibid.*

what may be called Kenya's state of mind at the beginning of the colonial era.

We could not know [she writes] and could not imagine, what the dangers were that they feared from our hands. I myself think that they were afraid of us more in the manner of a sudden terrific noise, than as you are afraid of suffering and death . . . perhaps they were, in life itself, within their own element, such as we can never be, like fishes in deep water which for the life of them cannot understand our fear of drowning. This assurance, this art of swimming, they had, I thought, because they had preserved a knowledge that was lost to us by our first parents; Africa, amongst the continents, will teach it to you: that God and the Devil are one, the majesty coeternal, not two uncreated but one uncreated, and the Natives neither confounded the person nor divided the substance. . . . All the time I felt the silent overshadowed existence of the Natives running parallel with my own, on a different plane. Echoes went from the one to the other. . . . The Natives were Africa in flesh and blood. . . . We ourselves, in our boots and in our constant hurry, often jar with the landscape. The Natives are in accordance with it, and when the tall, slim, dark, and dark-eyed people travel, — always one by one, so that even the great Native veins of traffic are narrow footpaths, — or work the soil, or herd their cattle, or hold their big dances, or tell you a tale, it is Africa wandering, dancing and entertaining you."[9]

The ritualistic dynamism of the dancing, however, was coming to an end as a simple act of worship, to be transformed into a noisy senseless treat for tourists with buzzing cameras.

Where had it gone, the psychic and physical energy of the Kenya African, as what has been described as a "great

[9] *Out of Africa*, Karen von Blixen.

hush" came over the country? As if mesmerized, the Africans watched the furious activities of the white man as he built railways, houses and roads, and tore away the bush to make his farms. Their wonder was mistaken for subservience. The old men shrugged their shoulders, their wonder limited by experience, and their displeasure moderated by age. For the young men, diverted from the traditional path of warriorhood and leadership into the new channels of literacy, Christianity, and the collar and tie, there was only one outlet — Nairobi. If they could not achieve manhood within the new culture they would find it nowhere else, and would remain as castaways adrift in a dying culture. Jomo Kenyatta was one of the first generation of Africans to make this bid for recognition. He, like far too many others, was to experience some appalling obstacles.

CHAPTER THREE

IT IS THE GRASS THAT SUFFERS

By THE time he went to Nairobi as a young man at the beginning of the Great War, Jomo Kenyatta had had an education based on both the traditional Kikuyu teachings and the new Western Christian model. "Like any other Gikuyu child," he wrote later, ". . . I acquired my country's equivalent of a liberal education."[1] Because the Kikuyu had no written language, education within the tribe was verbal, the grandparents taking a leading part in teaching the younger generation the tribal customs and traditions. Those of a similar age-group kept pace with each other in this learning, and for a culturally static society, which had to cope with an unceasingly repetitive pattern of problems, this education was a comprehensive one. Both male and female circumcision ceremonies initiated the boys and girls in sexual knowledge and responsibility, although female circumcision (involving excision of the clitoris) was a harsh practice which became the centre of bitter controversy.

"Following the tribal custom," wrote Kenyatta, "I had to pass through the several stages of initiation along with my age-group. . . . Although men do not witness the physical operation on the girls, they are not ignorant of its details, as the young initiates of both sexes talk freely to each other about it afterwards. Moreover, one of the operators was my aunt, Waco, and in visiting her homestead as a child, I

[1] *Facing Mount Kenya*, Preface, p. xvi.

naturally picked up the details of the process by hearing conversation between her and other women."[2]

A former missionary in Kikuyuland told me that she thought it was a pity that it was the Victorians, notoriously shy of sexual matters, who were the first British people to come to Kenya. Their emotional repugnance at some of the local customs helped to prevent a smooth transition to new ways.

The education which Kenyatta received at the Church of Scotland mission at the village of Kikuyu was, apart from the vocational side, mainly confined to the teaching of the Bible, English, and some mathematics. Being introduced to the wide complexity of Western civilization through these means, which for very good reasons of lack of time, staff and funds, largely ignored the historical process, tended to leave a large part of this dynamic new culture unexplained and almost incomprehensible. Unlike the young Englishman who, though perhaps having an equally sketchy academic education, would grow up within the existing product of history and thus understand it by precept, a young African could only understand it by what he learnt in the classroom, and by the actions of the Europeans with whom he came into contact — in other words, as an outsider. Not surprisingly, he would equate the teachings of the Bible and the beliefs of the missionaries in European society with the leading influence of the seers and divines in his own tribe. He was in no position to know that organized Christianity was just one aspect of the schizophrenic West and that many of the white men he would meet would be disciples of the god of utility. It is probable, judging by remarks made in his later years, that Jomo Kenyatta was no exception to the consequent con-

[2] *Ibid.*, p. xix.

fusion and disillusion which existed in the minds of many Africans.

An elderly Kikuyu civil servant described his impressions of this muddle of religion to me in the following terms, simply and without bitterness. "Formerly," he said, "we took every single European in this country to be a Christian, but when it did not appear so there was bound to be some confusion. I always maintain that the missionaries would have done a wonderful job here if they had not given in so often to the settlers. They preached a gospel which did not recognize a colour bar but there was a colour bar. I think if the European commercial life had been more Christian, Christianity would be much stronger here today." How could he, or Jomo Kenyatta, or the thousands of others who owed their knowledge of the Western world to the mission schools, know that the seers and divines of Europe had themselves lost the leadership of their people? The spirit of Europe was itself the hostage of superficial utilitarian and intellectual gods.

There is little doubt that much of the otherwise admirable missionary interest in Africa was due to the daunting obstacles which organized Christianity faced in Europe. In Africa there appeared to be an open field for religious teaching, and indeed the missionaries had it all their own way at first, owing partly to the intrinsic truth of the Gospels and partly to the marvellous powers of the white man which put white "magic" at a premium. Africa had to be introduced to Christianity if it was to survive in the modern world, and the chaos in Africa would have been worse if the god of utility had had the field to itself; but the missions suffered from a peculiarly Victorian vice. They did not introduce their pupils to the skeleton in their cupboard, the spiritual indifference of their own civilization. Nobody taught Jomo Kenyatta about the "dirt and gloom and squalor" that lay behind the "gold and purple robe of State." He found out for himself, later. As it was he entered the town life of Nairobi armed with the increasingly inadequate customs of tribal society and with a thin armour of Christian idealism. If what he wrote later was accurate he soon found out that what he had to deal with was not an integrated Christian society but the god of utility, usually faithfully attended by at least one "effective moral attitude."

Already Jomo Kenyatta had, according to his brother James, become something of a leader amongst his own age group. He used to wear a large hat with beads on it, and an embroidered belt. His brother did not know him very well at that time, being ten years younger, but from all accounts Jomo was something of a dandy, fond of dancing, and popular with the local girls. It was at about this time that he acquired the name Kenyatta, the Kikuyu word for a fancy belt. The small group of Africans in Nairobi with a mission education tended to stick together and thought of themselves, so James Muigai told me, as a "topclass" among the Africans, most of whom were employed as labourers and house servants. But the world of the Europeans was a long way off.

It was understandable that tribesmen with no knowledge of English or English ways should remain socially and physically apart, but, short of being reborn an Englishman, an African on the fringes of Western culture could not expect full membership either. House servants were, and still are, referred to as "boys," and those who, like Kenyatta, had had some schooling, were usually called "mission boys." The balance of psychological power was such at the time that this paternal attitude would doubtless

have been forgiven and forgotten if the "boys" had had a
chance of growing up. But if it was hard even for an Englishman to move up a class in his homeland, it was virtually
impossible for an African to do so in a colony. Preparations
were already well advanced to establish the colour bar,
which was to besiege the African in his own country for
the next fifty years. To understand some of the soul-eroding
finality of the colour bar it must be realised that, in a tribal
society, each member passed automatically from childhood to full adulthood through a series of initiation ceremonies, which ensured that added status was accompanied
by added responsibility. It was no joke to be faced with a
lifetime of suspended animation between the two societies.

As Jomo Kenyatta spent his days totting up figures for
his new master, and later reading meters for the Nairobi
Town Council, there was at least one chink in the white
wall before him, in the shape of a diminutive Scottish
engineer. W. McGregor Ross was soon to become Director
of Public Works in the Kenya Government and to spend
his twenty or more years as a civil servant buzzing around
the Heads of Government like an angry wasp. Like all the
best of his countrymen, he had a sharp eye for humbug
and was not afraid of exposing it. The book which he published on his retirement, *Kenya from Within*, is a lively
account of the sometimes grim, sometimes ludicrous, and
never dull, battle between the officials — who did their best
to safeguard what they honestly believed to be the "best
interests of the native," and the settlers, who fought with
great zest to prove that their fantasy was true, that Kenya
was a "white man's country." W. McGregor Ross's friendship must have been a valuable one. He was not one of
those "professional friends of the African," about whom
Kenyatta was to write so scathingly later, "who are pre-

pared to maintain their friendship for eternity as a sacred duty, provided only that the Africans will continue to play the part of an ignorant savage so that they can monopolise the office of interpreting his mind and speaking for him."[3]

Although James Muigai told me that his brother was "not interested in politics" during his first years in Nairobi, in the Great War, this state of mind did not last long, and from 1922, when Kenyatta joined the Young Kikuyu Association, politics were to dominate his life. To understand this period, culminating in his departure for England in 1929, it is necessary to fill in the general political background of Kenya's development.

In 1888 the Imperial British East Africa Company was granted a royal charter giving it a monopoly of trade over an area several times larger than Great Britain. The company was a strange mixture of businessmen, empire-builders, and idealists, and quickly found out that the moulding of such a vast region in the image of Britain was far beyond its resources. In 1895 the British Government stepped in and, by virtue of a whole host of peace treaties with the various tribes, declared the British East African Protectorate — to be redefined in 1920 as Kenya Colony and Protectorate. The first problem which faced the British Government was what to do with this enormous piece of territory to justify its acquisition in the eyes of the British Parliament. Imperialism was all very grand, and it looked important on the map, but there were plenty of hardheaded taxpayers who could not see any use in putting money into imperialism unless something came out of it. After much debate, plans for a railway to encourage trade and ensure an adequate defence were drawn up. By 1901 the first train steamed into Kisumu on the shores of Lake

[3] *Ibid.*, p. xviii.

Victoria. But the "iron snake," or the "twin ribbons of rust," depending on the point of view, seemed to create more problems than it solved.

The Uganda Railway was an epic of Victorian romance, and even today, in an age which expects scientific miracles daily, the passenger from Mombasa to Kampala in Uganda must be very dull not to appreciate a little of the energy and perseverance which created this trade route. He leaves Mombasa in the evening, and during the night the train rumbles through wild barren country, where the engineers and railway workers had to compete with the heat and man-eating lions. In the morning he wakes to find the air cooler, and as he has breakfast he can watch giraffe, ostrich, zebra, wildebeest, and gazelle as they graze on the wide open plains. Nairobi is soon reached and the air there is warm but dry. Then the train winds in and out of the Kikuyu valleys as it climbs up to a height of more than seven thousand feet at the edge of the Rift Valley. It sidles down the wall of the valley, offering enormous views over plains occupied by acacia trees, Masai herdsmen with their droves of cattle, and wild game. Next begins the slow climb up again into some of the most fertile parts of the White Highlands, with park-like scenery which might have been borrowed from England. At nine thousand feet the air is sharp and thin, even under an equatorial sun, and there may be a frost as the train puffs across the Equator at night. Then, later, Lake Victoria comes into sight in the distance, thousands of feet below and shimmering whitely in the sunlight, and as the train descends towards it, the air becomes thicker and warmer. Finally Uganda is reached and the last lap is through tall dark forest and tropical green cultivation. The Victorians, however, wanted more than a scenic railway for their 5½ million pounds.

The old British East Africa Company had a regulation limiting the alienation and sale of land to Europeans, but under the inspiration of Sir Charles Eliot (Commissioner for the East African Protectorate, 1901–4) the handful of settlers began to increase rapidly. Sir Charles suffered from no illusions about "civilizing missions," and said openly: "The interior of the Protectorate is a white man's country, and it is mere hypocrisy not to admit that white interests must be paramount, and the main object of our policy should be to found a white colony." But he added, "To say that European interests must be paramount does not mean that any violence or hostility should be shown to natives." He recognized accurately that it was the Kikuyu district ". . . where the land question is likely to present real difficulties. . . ."[4]

According to the Carter Commission which investigated the tangled land problem in 1932, the Kikuyu tribe occupied an area of 1519 square miles before the white man came to Kenya. According to the same Commission, the area of Kikuyu land alienated for the use of settlers, near Nairobi, was 109 square miles. Even if there is some margin of error in these figures it is clear that the question of land, upon which the political storm in Kenya has been centered, was far more than a matter of acres of red soil.

It has been seen that land played, and still plays, an essential part in the religious and social, as well as the economic aspects of Kikuyu tribal life. The cry "They have stolen our land" was at root a cry against a new and dominant culture, and is a common denominator in most colonial nationalism. It is a defensive reflex, a last-ditch stand in defence of the "good old days." The fact that the Carter Commission awarded other land as compensation, even if

[4] *Ibid.*, p. 104.

that land was not as acceptable, made no difference whatever to the accusation. In fact, by the time of the Mau Mau rebellion in 1952, the entire White Highlands were said to have been "stolen" — an area of 16,000 square miles. Land itself was not the reason why the Europeans made themselves more and more disliked. When the transition from the tribal to the Western way of life was seen to be hedged with crippling qualifications, it is not surprising that many turned back and fought with the only weapons they had, the weapons of their tribal beliefs. The only men who could have prevented this regression, those who had had some education in Western ways, were the ones most sensitive to the obstacles in their way, and retreat for them was the ultimate hell.

As early as 1902 Colonel Meinertzhagen, who served with the King's African Rifles, wrote: ". . . the Kikuyu are ripe for trouble, and when they get educated and medicine men are replaced by political agitators, there will be a general rising." Later, in 1904, he made another assessment. "They are intelligent," he wrote, "and I can see that with education they will turn out to be a great asset to East Africa, provided we do not let them brood over grievances." Not only were they allowed to brood but new grievances were added for good measure.

By 1903 there were about one hundred settlers, mostly near Nairobi, on land to which the Kikuyu laid claim, despite the fact that a Crown Ordinance promulgated the previous year had laid down that ". . . in all dealings with the Crown regard shall be had to the rights and requirements of the natives and in particular the Commissioner shall not sell or lease any land in actual occupation of the natives." But the snag came in the last phrase of this apparently worthy law. "Occupation" was interpreted as synonymous with "cultivation," and compensation was offered at the rate of two rupees an acre. Individual rights were not acknowledged. This meant either that land near Nairobi owned by individual Kikuyu, but temporarily abandoned after the disasters already mentioned, was considered legally unoccupied, or that the tribe as a whole received the meagre compensation for it. But, however unjust this may have been, it remains true that this injustice in itself could not have led to so much trouble if it had not been aggravated by other and deeper injustices. Nothing happened in Kenya remotely comparable with the cavalier manner in which the Red Indians were shot and argued off their land in North America. But times had changed and it was increasingly difficult, no matter how carefully it was done, to occupy land in a strange country and justify it in the eyes of those concerned, or the world outside.

In 1903 it looked as if Kenya were about to become a back garden for the House of Lords in London. Lord Delamere got 100,000 acres, the Earl of Portsmouth, 350,000 acres, and Lord Francis Scott took up another vast estate, as did Ewart Grogan. A suggestion made in London that part of Kenya should become a new home for the Jews was greeted with an urgent telegram: "Is it for this that the expensive railway was built and large sums spent on the country? Flood of people of that class is sure to lead to trouble with half-tamed natives jealous of their rights. Have we no colonists of our own race?" Kenya was to be kept for the "old school tie" set.

Defenders of the settlers, and they have had such able supporters as Elspeth Huxley, point to the enterprise of the early pioneers, to the hardships which they suffered before their farms were established, and to the personal fortunes which some of them, notably Lord Delamere, poured into

their efforts. This is true, but as a later Governor, Sir Philip
Mitchell, himself now a settler, said:

"... The colonist was himself, although no doubt seldom
conscious of it, a very different man from his forefathers
who drove the Red Indians from the fertile lands of North
America, a man with far greater and more complicated
wants and far less self-sufficiency. He was not, in fact, a
colonist at all in their sense. For he had neither the inten-
tion nor the capacity to live by the land, by his own labour
and that of his family, by his axe, his plough and his rifle.
He meant to employ others and to depend largely on imported goods, and he was much more akin to the tea
planter in Ceylon than to the colonist in Australia, Canada
or New Zealand."[5]

By 1907 a nominated Legislative Council was established, with six officials and two (later four) settlers. The
first African to appear in the Legislative Council was nominated after the Second World War, by Sir Philip Mitchell.
In order to persuade the Africans to leave their homes and
work on white farms the settlers put pressure on the Government to raise the taxes so that money would have to be
earned. By 1918 the African hut and poll tax realised
280,000 pounds and the "non-native" poll tax (there was
no income tax then) brought in 12,197 pounds. In the 1918
estimates for Government expenditure 1940 pounds were
set aside for agricultural instruction and seed for the African reserves. In the same year a scheme put forward by the
Chief Native Commissioner to compel Africans to make
better use of their land was shelved after the settlers had
protested for labour reasons. The greater the number of
settlers, the greater was the pressure brought to bear on
the Government to govern in the interests of the settlers,

[5] *The Agrarian Problem in Kenya*, 1947, Sir Philip Mitchell, p. 4.

using the African population as the working class of England had been used for many years, as a convenient source of labour. No concerted effort was to be made to help the Africans to develop their own land until it was almost too late, nearly fifty years later.

For the next years, until well after the Great War, Kenya hovered on the brink of forced labour as an official policy to drive African peasants out of their reserves to work on settler farms. Although there were many examples of official pressure being put on the local people to "encourage" them to go out to work, the Kenya Government never quite gave in to the loud and insistent demands of the settlers. Some District Commissioners, most of whom were far better educated than the average settler and often developed a fierce paternal affection for those under their influence, did their best to prevent compulsion. An example was the D.C. of North Kavirondo, near Lake Victoria, who wrote in a memorandum: "If we proceed to a comparison of conditions of labour in the settled and native areas, it can, I think, be established that in his own area the native is in the main better fed, better housed, is not driven to choose between celibacy and syphilis, . . . and without working in all weathers under an overseer, can make sufficient for his simple needs." The Great War provided a brief respite as far as this issue was concerned, but it created other problems.

Europe's growing addiction to aggressive competition, which had been temporarily appeased by the unresisting compliance of Africa to her will, finally turned inward upon herself, and in 1914 the young men of Britain, France, and Germany went out to shoot each other down or die of disease in Flanders mud. Ripples of this wave of insanity reached East Africa, and soon the British and Ger-

man colonials were doing their best to emulate their relatives. By comparison the result was inept, and occasionally
brightened by moments of old-fashioned chivalry, as when
the captain of a ship of the Royal Navy warned the port
of Tanga, occupied by Germans, to evacuate before he
launched an attack. The German reaction was to strew the
approach to the town, which lay through thick bush, with
trip-wires attached to beehives. The Germans stayed in
Tanga, and the English steamed away, stung to the quick
by this teutonic *schadenfreude*.

Meanwhile thousands of Africans were recruited as
porters and duly followed their patriotic white masters
backwards and forwards through the bush in support of
their war. *Punch* cartoonists would have revelled in this
amusing pattern of black and white had it not been for
the fact that large numbers of the porters — figures up to
twenty thousand have been quoted — died of disease before the survivors could return home to their families. It
would have required a good many years of tribal fighting
to equal this total. A Swahili proverb covered the situation
neatly: "When two elephants fight it is the grass that suf-
fers."

The end of the war saw an immediate increase in tension
between black and white, and for the first time the Indian
population, already more than twice the size of the white
community, began to make its presence felt politically.
During this war the veils had been partially lifted from
the mysteries of State, and some of the younger Africans
had seen something of what lay behind. White supremacy
could no longer be taken for granted. It had to be repeat-
edly affirmed. The Europeans themselves, like Europe, had
been badly shaken by the war, as was evidenced by their

near-hysterical political behaviour during the next few years.

The fight by the settlers to get at the land and labour of the Africans was more or less held in check by the Government — but this did little to help the insecurity of the local people. In 1915 a Crown Lands Ordinance had extended the settler's lease of land to 999 years, and had laid down that all land held by Africans was to be classified as Crown land. One purpose of this was to safeguard it against sale to Europeans, but the effect was to make the Africans tenants of the Crown, which aggravated their sense of insecurity. They asked for legal guarantees of ownership, but it was not until after the Second World War that title deeds, or "tiddlydee" as they were called, were granted.

In 1917 an Economic Commission (known to the impious as the Comic Commission) had been set up, consisting mainly of settlers, including Lord Delamere and Ewart (now Major) Grogan. It reported in 1919 and contained a tirade against Indian businessmen and Indians in general. It was rejected by both the House of Commons and the House of Lords, and was described as "purely deplorable" by Lord Milner. A further source of insecurity for many Africans was the "squatter" system whereby many landless Africans drifted onto European farms and were allowed to use a small patch of land in return for their labour. This placed them firmly in the power of the farmer, and they became as dependent on the character of the farmer concerned as the serfs of England in feudal times on the good will of their masters. The system was wide open to abuse and the Resident Native's Ordinance of 1918 attempted to legalize it by introducing contract terms and safeguards regarding work and powers of dismissal. But, as so often happened in Kenya, it was merely a good-natured effort to make a thoroughly unsatisfactory system tolerable. A radical reform, such as allowing a number of Africans to own land near white farms, was not even discussed.

In 1920 a Registration Act, passed in 1915, was enforced, laying down that every male over sixteen years must carry a certificate of identity incorporating an employment record. No man could get a job until his previous employer had signed a certificate of discharge. The idea behind this, supported by the settlers, was that it would stop "deserting" from contracts. It also meant that the employer's grip on his labour tightened still further, and it was as universally hated as the pass laws in South Africa were later to become. The average pay of a farm labourer at this time was about ten shillings per month, and a month often consisted of thirty days' work. Hut tax in 1922 amounted to twelve shillings per year. A man with a family might have three huts, or more.

To confound these moves to attach the African firmly to the requirements of a cash economy, the economy itself began to collapse. Known to its enemies as "anarchy plus one policeman," the economic system of the West moved into a postwar slump, and Kenya farmers suddenly found that they had more labour than they wanted. The African worker found himself attached to a sinking ship. He was taxed, he was barred from growing such valuable crops as coffee, he risked being dismissed as redundant, and he had no representation in the Government. The settlers, who by now had won a controlling voice in Government expenditures, then proposed a reduction in African wages of one third — from ten shillings to seven. At this point the worm turned — but only to be quickly suppressed once more.

On June 11, 1921, a letter appeared in the local Nairobi daily written by a young Kikuyu who worked for the Treasury as a telephone operator. It read:

"A meeting of the proposed Young Kikuyu Association was held at Pangani village on Tuesday, when the subject was the native wages reduction. It was proposed and carried unanimously that the rules of the Association should be drawn and forwarded to the Government. . . . It was also suggested and carried that, in order to show the native grievances to the Government in the matter of wages reduction schemed by the farmers of the Colony, the Association, though still on proposal, is in the position of writing to the Hon. Chief Native Commissioner, asking him to lay the matter before His Excellency the Governor."

The writer was Harry Thuku, and his letter was to set in train a progression of events which will not culminate until Kenya is an independent state. It is doubtful whether Harry Thuku, in 1960 an elderly and successful farmer with little interest in politics, guessed the implications of his action. The Government and the settlers certainly did not. Harry Thuku belonged to that small but growing "top-class" of mission-educated Africans, mainly Kikuyu, who occupied lower clerical posts in Nairobi. It was at this time that Jomo Kenyatta began to concern himself with politics, and he joined the new association.

Following this letter a meeting was held a couple of weeks later just outside Nairobi at the village of Dagoretti — where Lugard had once built a fort, subsequently burnt down by the Kikuyu. The meeting may confidently be added to that endless list of the world's "historical turning points," and was described by the Director of Public Works, W. McGregor Ross.

Senior Government Officials were there from Nairobi [he wrote], District Officers, missionaries, Kikuyu chiefs and attendants, natives in red paint, mission boys and members of the Young Kikuyu Association in imported clothing — the old order and the new, in the native world; the Government insisted upon respect for the recognized (and salaried) chiefs and headmen; younger men, acting in *combination*, thrusting themselves in between the paid chiefs and the Government, and claiming the attention which organization always elicits. A portent.

The young men acted and spoke with a composure and self-confidence that grated upon the paid chiefs. These young men were partially educated. They had attended mission schools (the only ones in existence) for the sake of getting some education. Under the glib classification of the average white immigrant, they were "mission boys." To the missionaries many of them were known "failures," who had responded little or not at all to mission influence, but had only snatched the coveted boon of education which the mission offered free, and had then decamped with it. To the missionaries (as a body) they were an object of suspicion tinged with resentment. To the Government they were a probable source of embarrassment. To the paid chiefs they were anathema. Nobody wanted them or wanted to meet them. And here they were, forcing a hearing. They were supported by some of the headmen. Behind the sullen demeanour that the Kikuyu so readily adopts when he has a grievance, real or imaginary, these natives were boiling hot.

They complained of forced labour of girls and young women. . . . "When we went to do war work we were told by His Excellency the Governor that we should be rewarded, but is our reward to have our tax raised and to have registration papers given to us and for our ownership of our land to be called into question; to be told today that we are to receive title deeds and tomorrow for it to appear that we are not to receive them?"[6]

[6] *Kenya from Within,* W. McGregor Ross, p. 225.

Government said it would consider the matter. Harry Thuku was told that he must choose between his job and politics, and chose politics.

It would be wrong to think that the whole Kikuyu tribe was in a political ferment. Most of them were living peacefully enough in the twilight of their traditional society, but their initiative had been taken away by the Government, and no matter how wise the District Commissioners might be, they could not be an effective substitute. The Kikuyu people became like dried grass, waiting to be set alight by men who could lead them to a new self-respect. By 1960 a District Commissioner was able to write that at heart every Kikuyu was a nationalist. But in 1921 the only independence talked about was by settlers determined to lay their own hands on the government of the country, and run it their own way.

To the startled Government, the sacked telephone operator looked as if he were determined to bring it down. Men who had hardly got used to the life of universal suffrage in England were amazed to see that Kenya's working class too was human, and knew what was in its interest quite as well as its mentors. Meetings were held; a shilling a month was collected from supporters (who were earning between seven and ten shillings a month), leaflets were printed, promises made, telegrams sent to the King of England, and cars were hired to tour the reserves. Crowds of up to five thousand people cheered the speakers. The Europeans were being challenged at their own game of political agitation.

Gradually, as Government did not respond to the demands, the speeches got more and more heated. At one meeting Harry Thuku suggested loading three hired lorries with identity cards and dumping them in the drive of Government House. This successor to the Boston Tea Party never materialised, however. The official spirits of "peace and good order" were invoked by an irritated Government, and on March 15 (the Ides of March) Harry Thuku was arrested. A riot developed outside the prison in Nairobi and a trigger-happy policeman touched off a fusillade which resulted in twenty-five deaths. News spread quickly to the reserves that a massacre had occurred. This first sacrifice on the altar of Kenya nationalism was carried out, not in a heroic, but in an almost pantomime setting. An eye-witness said that a number of "gaudily dressed native women, mostly town prostitutes, were the noisiest element there," and an English chaplain said the scene before the shooting reminded him of a "Sunday School treat," despite the fact that some of the women are reported to have flung themselves screaming round his neck when the firing started.

Harry Thuku passed, without trial, into political oblivion for the next eight years, exiled to one of those dusty northern outposts which the Kenya Government was to use for a similar purpose in later years. African political organization had proved itself for the first time. In the words of Jomo Kenyatta, written later: "But the idea of union had taken hold of the people's imagination, and instead of being killed the Association was driven underground . . . The Africans of Kenya had their Maquis long before Hitler appeared on the European scene."[7]

It was perhaps inevitable that the new educated African elite should use political agitation as a successor to the old initiation rites and as a proving ground in the Western world, but it was a pity that the Government proved incapable of governing successfully that small but vital

[7] *Kenya, Land of Conflict*, Kenyatta, London, Panaf Service, p. 11.

number of "mission boys." In the official inquiry that followed the riot, the Chief Native Commissioner made a remark which is a sad commentary on official understanding. He thought that the main theme of Harry Thuku's movement was to "stimulate enmity between black and white and to get the people to consider that they are in a state of slavery which has been imposed upon them by the Europeans."[8] This superficial appreciation was to have a long line of equally undistinguished successors during the coming years.

The Young Kikuyu Association remained inactive for some time after this blow, but was then revived under the name of the Kikuyu Central Association, led by Joseph Kangethe and Jesse Kariuki. In 1925 it petitioned the Governor for permission to grow coffee; for the appointment of a Kikuyu paramount chief; for the publication of the laws of Kenya in the Kikuyu language; and for the release of Harry Thuku. It received its support, not from the bulk of the people in the reserves, but from those in Nairobi, and from the landless "squatters" on settler farms, now numbering over 100,000. It was an attempt to find a legitimate voice for those Kikuyu who had come directly in contact with the white man's world. Compared with the settler's title-studded and noisy political organization, it was a feeble pressure group indeed, ill-organized and, by English standards, half-educated. If it had been wisely handled and encouraged there is no reason why it could not have found an appropriate place in Kenya society. But against the settler belief that might and class were right, and against Government indifference and then hostility, it began to degenerate into a desperate face-saving campaign, involving bitterness to the Europeans who had followed up

[8] Command Paper 1691 (1922), pp. 3–4.

their promises with snubs. But even then the situation was
far from hopeless, and, as with a jilted lover, there was
more than a small desire for reconciliation in the African
heart.

Jomo Kenyatta became an official of the Kikuyu Central
Association in 1925, and three years later he took up political work as a "full-time job." He became editor of a news-
sheet in the same year: it was called *Mwigwithania*,
which means "reconciler," and had as its motto, "Pray and
Work." It was badly printed, but aimed, according to a
Kikuyu friend who used to read it, at "uniting the masses
and teaching them how to help themselves." It also
preached the battle cry of all African politicians from then
on: "Give us back our land." However, the K.C.A. and this
particular paper received a good word in the Native Affairs Department report for 1928: "It is energetic, virile
and enterprising and among its other activities publishes a
monthly newspaper in Kikuyu, *Mwigwithania*, the contents
of which have been for the most part quite unexceptionable
and deserving of much commendation." But no matter how
energetic and commendable, the infant African pressure
group made no dent on Government policy or settler in-
transigence.

During the twenties, apart from the Thuku riot, the Government had its hands full trying to cope with the settlers,
who had increased in number to 15,000. An influx of ex-
army officers had arrived after the war and perhaps it was
this martial element which egged on what nearly turned
into an epic of "pantomime" slapstick. What became known
as the "Indian Question" flared up in the early twenties and
nearly led to a desperate attempt by the settlers to kidnap
the Governor and carry out a *coup d'état*. Winston Churchill, as Colonial Secretary, made a speech in which he de-

clared that, "so far as is practical," his Government would grant equal civil and political rights to all "civilized men," and it was proposed that a modest beginning should be made with a common roll in the new constitution. These unambitious proposals led to uproar and near anarchy.

Nobody worried about the Africans, who were not deemed to be within centuries of qualifying on these terms. It was the Indian community, now outnumbering the whites by three to one, which became the target of the "pukka sahibs" of the White Highlands. At Limuru, a few miles from Nairobi, a former resident of India said apoplectically: "Certainly there are a number of decent Indians in India, but in this Colony they are too awful for words." "The cunning of the Oriental" was exposed by the settlers' loudspeaker, the Convention of Associations, which warned its members to beware of the "tentacles of this evil menace." Some panic-stricken women sent a cable to Queen Mary saying: "We, the women of Kenya, humbly implore your assistance to protect us and our children from the terrible Asiatic menace which threatens to overwhelm us."

Pious phrases were dusted and thrown into the fray. In a petition to the King of England the settlers suggested hopefully that he must view with "peculiar concern the possibility that the flower of Christian Faith . . . may be choked by the quick growth of other Eastern religions . . . and that work done in the past by Christian pioneers may be lost." Bishops and archdeacons joined in the battle, some on one side and some on the other. Lord Delamere put on his stiff collar and jumped in at the pious end: "Our concern for our people in Kenya and the well-being of the native people does not blind us to the fact that the danger to the Empire and Christianity is greater." The heavens must have laughed at his impudence. In desperation, a plot was hatched to kidnap the Governor, in the name of the King, and to threaten the British Government with a colonial rebellion. The threat worked, and the common roll was abandoned. This attempt to exorcise racialism gradually from Kenya was a complete failure, thanks to settler nationalism.

Lord Delamere and his friends were pleased when the then Colonial Secretary, the Duke of Devonshire, masked his undignified retreat with what became a key statement on British colonial policy in Kenya. "His Majesty's Government," said the Duke, "record their considered opinion that the interests of the African natives must be paramount, and that if and when those interests and those of the immigrant races should conflict, the former should prevail." The settlers, whose minds were preoccupied with "Oriental cunning," failed to realise that this statement would later become a stout stick in the hands of African leaders. However, they were to wait many years before these fine words were put into effect.

There were of course settlers who preferred farming to political hysteria, but their influence was not felt. In the whole miserable incident there was at least one breath of common sense, from the Indian representatives. "We think it safest," they said, "and best in the present circumstances, that neither the Indian nor the European settler should have the control of native affairs, and that the legislative power should be taken out of their hands and kept in the hands of the Imperial Government till a time in the future when the African native is sufficiently advanced in education and intelligence to manage his own affairs and rule over his own country."

With frantic effort the settlers had bought a respite from the laws of common decency, at a price which they paid in lack of respect from those who watched their political antics from close quarters. The Director of Public Works made a characteristically shrewd comment: "The habit of life of some Europeans seems to have atrophied their intuitive faculties to the extent of allowing them to believe that it would be possible to maintain a white colony, in residence in a climate and land where the services of black men are required at every turn, by the threat of armed correction for any laxity in meeting their requirements. . . ."

To those Kikuyu who had turned their faces from the age-old snows of Kere-Nyaga towards the puzzling din of Nairobi there was only one lesson to be learnt from the undignified ways of settler politics. White supremacy, in the sense that every white man was thought to embody the dynamic truths of Western civilization, was dying, though it was to linger on, surprisingly enough, for a few more years. The young African who wished to succeed in this brawling society knew he had somehow to gain the power to enforce his will in the face of strong competition. In 1929 Jomo Kenyatta persuaded the Kikuyu Central Association to send him to London to present Kikuyu grievances to what was considered by them a more benevolent institution than the Kenya Government.

CHAPTER FOUR

GENTLEMEN OF THE JUNGLE

Now IN his early thirties Jomo Kenyatta arrived in England in February 1929. With him was an Indian lawyer from Kenya called Isher Dass. *The Times* of February 21 declared that the purpose of his visit was to "interview the Secretary of State on problems affecting the Kikuyu tribe, especially the land question." Also included in the petition, according to the Corfield Report, was a request that there should be direct elections by Africans of their own representatives for the Legislative Council in Nairobi, and that "ultimately the number of African representatives in Legislative Council should predominate."[1]

The dignity of the Colonial Office was shaken by this unprecedented impudence. Like well-behaved Victorian children, colonies were expected to be seen (on the map) but not heard. After much hurried consultation and adjusting of stiff collars, the petition was not permitted to reach the Colonial Secretary direct from the hands of the colonial, but he eventually saw it by devious means. Apart from some comment in the papers, nothing was done about it.

Although bitterly disappointed at this frigid reception, Jomo Kenyatta was not without friends and supporters. He was helped and advised, immediately after his arrival, by

[1] *Report on the Origins and Growth of Mau Mau*, Government Printers, Nairobi, 1960.

Charles Freer Andrews, a Church of England missionary, and William McGregor Ross, Kenya's former Director of Public Works, who had by now retired from service in Kenya. McGregor Ross and his wife did much to help Kenyatta during his first few difficult months in England.

One organization that immediately helped him was the League against Imperialism, formed two years earlier under Communist inspiration. The League arranged for Kenyatta to address meetings and gave him as much financial aid as its meagre resources permitted. Reginald Bridgeman, who was the secretary of the League at that time, was deeply impressed by Kenyatta's burning sincerity and single-mindedness. His descriptions of the harsh pass laws in Kenya, and the land hunger of the Kikuyu, aroused the sympathy and indignation of the League, but some members of it were disappointed at his apparently complete lack of interest in the wider issue of colonialism. According to Bridgeman, Kenyatta knew nothing about any other colony, and seemed uninterested in widening his views beyond the narrow perspective of his tribe.

This criticism seems a little unjust when it is considered that Kenyatta's education, apart from that gained within the tribe, was not of the kind to give him a perspective of world affairs. Socialism also held little interest for him at this stage, and he and the League quickly became disillusioned with each other. Bridgeman found Kenyatta less likeable than the West Africans with whom he had to deal, and he felt that Kenyatta's proper place was in Kenya where there was a real need for leadership of his people. In his own words, he thought that Kenyatta "seemed to lose his fire."

For his part, Jomo Kenyatta, seeing that the League could do little to help him, lost interest in it and became associated with George Padmore, the West Indian Trade Unionist, who had himself become divorced from the League's activities. Later the two men were to play an important part together in the organization of the Pan-African Federation in 1945.

In August of the year of his arrival Kenyatta paid the first of many visits to the continent of Europe, and the first of two he was to pay to the U.S.S.R. Unfortunately there is nothing to indicate what impression the ways of Moscow had on Kenyatta during this visit, but he did not stay long, and by October of that year he was back in England. Shortly afterwards he attended the International Negro Workers' Conference in Hamburg and then went on to meet a number of leading Communists in Berlin.

This flirtation with Communism should be seen in perspective. At that time, when working-class people in industrialised countries lived a miserable life in smoke-ridden cities, and when economic control was a virtually unknown art, many people looked desperately for a way out. Communism offered a coherent plan which aimed to subordinate money to brotherhood and need, and many intelligent people swallowed the bait. There is no evidence at all that Kenyatta ever developed any deep conviction for, or understanding of, the complex theories of Marxism, despite the fact that the Corfield Report (p. 42) claims that he joined the Communist Party soon after his return from Moscow.

Early in 1930, on March 26, Kenyatta had a letter accepted by the *Times* in which he outlined his political aims. The letter followed a correspondence on education and unrest in Kenya in which Julian Huxley took part. It is worth quoting in full:

To the Editor of *The Times:*

Sir, May I be permitted to throw some light on the so-called "Unrest among Kikuyu Natives" referred to recently in your paper? I should mention, *en passant*, that I am a Kikuyu, and, with all public-spirited men of my tribe, regard with considerable uneasiness the policy which is being advocated by certain influential people, both in Kenya and in this country, of further alienating our land from us, for the use of non-natives, in conjunction with attempts to abolish wholesale our tribal customs. General Smuts has recently condemned most wholeheartedly a similar policy which is being carried out in South Africa.

The K.C.A., of which I am the General Secretary, is not a subversive organization. Its object is to help the Kikuyu to improve himself as a Mu-Kikuyu — not to "ape" the foreigner. Our aims and objects may be summarized briefly under the following five headings:—

1 Land. To obtain a legal right recognized by the local government to the tenure of the lands held by our tribe before the advent of the foreigner, and to prevent further encroachment by non-natives on the Native Reserves.

2 Education. To obtain educational facilities of a practical nature to be financed by a portion of the taxes paid by us to the Government.

3 Women's Hut Tax. To obtain the abolition of the Hut Tax on women — which leads to their being forced to work outside the Native Reserves, or into prostitution for the purpose of obtaining money to pay this tax.

4 Representation in the Legislature. To obtain the representation of native interests on the Legislative Council, by native representatives elected by themselves.

5 Tribal Customs. To be permitted to retain our many good tribal customs, and by means of education to elevate the minds of our people to the willing rejection of the bad customs.

Evolving from these points, we hope to remove all lack of understanding between the various races who form the population of East Africa, so that we may all march together as loyal subjects of His Britannic Majesty along the road to Empire prosperity. I would like to ask if any fair-minded Briton considers the above outlined policy of the K.C.A. to savour in any way of sedition? The repression of native views, on subjects of such vital interest to my people, by means of legislative measures, can only be described as a short-sighted tightening up of the safety valve of free speech, which must inevitably result in a dangerous explosion — the one thing all sane men wish to avoid.

Johnstone Kenyatta, General Secretary, K.C.A.,
95, Cambridge St., London, S.W.I.

Twenty-two years later the explosion occurred, for lack of a safety valve.

By September 1930, his money having run out, Jomo Kenyatta returned to Kenya. Politically he had achieved little more than a few fleeting second thoughts in Whitehall, but personally he had learnt a lot. He had seen the white man on his home ground, the launching site of the "civilizing mission" of which he had hitherto seen only the target area. He had left Kenya little more than an intelligent but ill-educated tribesman. Europe, for all its confusion, and partly because of it, was a challenging place, and Jomo Kenyatta was obviously not sorry that he was soon to return. But the need to relate himself and his people to the world outside had become even more urgent.

Kenyatta was welcomed on his return to Nairobi by family, friends, and officials of the K.C.A. His visit to Europe had given him added stature in the eyes of his people, but Harry Thuku, still under Government auspices miles away in a remote area, was considered by many to be the senior leader. In the curious world of colonial politics, prison can be a surer step up the ladder of popularity than visits to the seat of authority in distant lands. Margaret, Kenyatta's eldest daughter and nowadays a mature woman with large sad eyes and a rare but infectious laugh, was a very young girl in those days but she can remember a little of her father at this time. "I can remember the crowds of people who used to visit him at home, and I often used to make him play with me and he held me up in front of the people and they all laughed."

Among his visitors then were members of a new religious sect called the Watu wa Mungu (the People of God). The sect was the result of the spiritual confusion which had come with the wholesale introduction of Christianity into the delicately balanced tribal pattern of belief. It sought to unite tribal and Christian beliefs and retained customs like polygamy, female circumcision, and ancestor worship. It was a desperate attempt to find some sort of spiritual independence in a bewildering world, and the leaders claimed to have direct contact with God. All things foreign, apart from certain aspects of Christianity, were regarded as unclean. It was a short step from spiritual "nationalism" to a more political line. After considering them at first to be, in Kenyatta's words, "simply a bunch of lunatics,"[2] the Government began to watch their activities, and some were arrested for incitement to violence. This rather pathetic spiritual retreat catered for the many who had left their own customs but had been unable to find a home within one of the many expressions of Christianity which were offered to them. In the days leading up to Mau Mau this retreat became a rout.

With the security of their land uncertain, their religion

[2] *Facing Mount Kenya*, p. 277.

challenged, and a battle going on above their heads about
the possibility of federating East Africa (with the prospect of white dominion for eternity) tension was increasing
among the African people. A missionary told me recently
that the atmosphere was almost as tense as later during
Mau Mau. The police discovered that Kikuyu clerks in
government service were acting as spies for the K.C.A. But
the rumble of approaching thunder died away again.

The then Governor of Kenya, Sir Edward Grigg (later
Lord Altrincham), a man of strong religious convictions
and a great capacity for groundless optimism, later wrote
of his "strongest impression" of life in Kenya being the
"happiness of relations between mixed races" there.[3] He
considered that "native unrest" was merely "propaganda
thrust upon the life of the Colony from ignorant sources
outside."[4] Similar explanations are still echoing around the
world today, in places which would have astonished Lord
Altrincham. He shared another delusion with many others
of his time, namely, that Africans were "so primitive that
for civilizing purposes they are almost a clean slate."[5]
Only the faintest tremors from the political, economic, and
spiritual earthquakes of Europe were allowed to disturb
the calm of Government House, Nairobi.

Only six months after Kenyatta's return to Kenya the
K.C.A. decided to send its own representatives to London, to present its views to the Parliamentary Joint Committee on Closer Union in East Africa. Many Africans
feared that a union of the three East African territories of
Kenya, Uganda, and Tanganyika would result in a South
African type of government, independent of London. There
was still a widespread belief that if only the British Gov-

[3] *Kenya's Opportunity*, Lord Altrincham, p. 294.
[4] *Ibid.*   [5] *Ibid.*, p. 286.

ernment would understand their viewpoint all would be
well. And in the end, after much muddle and misunder-
standing and some wisdom, the idea of closer union was
dropped.

Jomo Kenyatta, and another Kikuyu, Parmenas Githen-
du Mockerie, were chosen to go to London, and on April
28, 1931, the two of them set out from Nairobi. A glimpse
of what it meant in those days to be a "mission boy," attempting to penetrate the Western world with inadequate
resources, is given by one of the travellers, Parmenas
Mockerie.

A crowd of a thousand people came to see us off. It was
very difficult for all the town workers to buy platform tickets which cost ten cents (one shilling is one hundred
cents) because they had spent their last month's earnings,
and most of them would be in debt, expecting to repay
when they got their wages at the end of the month. But
those who were able to get the tickets came onto the platform and stood in rows of five deep. The president of the
Association, then Mr. Joseph Kangethe, gave a short talk
to the crowd, explaining to the people the reasons why the
K.C.A. had decided to send their delegates to England.
Among the crowd were a few Indians and a white detec-
tive. One of the Indians discouraged me while I was shak-
ing hands with people on the platform by saying to me,
"How can these poor people succeed in their struggles;
don't they realize that only money talks?" This made me
think that the Indian was an enemy of our cause, but I
realised later when I arrived in England that he was trying
to give me a hint. I replied to him that although money
talks, the committee which we were going to see treated
the representatives of the poor in the same manner as
those of the rich. He may have had some experience of
British politics in the past of which I had no knowledge . . .
On our way in the train we ordered supper and asked for a
table to be provided in the dining-car for both of us. The

steward told us that as we were Africans (we were travelling second-class) we were not entitled to use the dining-car, which was reserved for Europeans. He said the meal could be brought to our carriage and we could eat it there . . . It was very late when he brought the supper, and when I tasted the soup it made me feel sick, as it was very cold. . . .[6]

Victorian class consciousness was degenerating in Kenya into something close to the insane master-race theory which was then beginning to eat into the German mentality in Europe. There can be very few educated Africans alive even today who have not been subjected on occasions to trivial jibes at their dignity such as the incident recounted above. But Kenyatta and his friend had not yet run the gauntlet of colonial manners. When their ship, the Italian steamer *Mazzini*, called at the main port of Italian Somalia, Kenyatta and his companion went ashore. They tried to get a taxi to take them round the town, but taxis were for Europeans only, and on trying to walk down one street they were told by a policeman that that too was for Europeans. However, at Massawa, a small Italian colony on the Red Sea, they were pleasantly surprised to find that Africans were accepted in the hotels.

On the boat itself, Parmenas recalls, they were well treated by the European passengers, "except by a missionary who had been in Kikuyu for sixteen years and was going to Italy for furlough. We had a little quarrel with him when he told us to stand up when a European was strolling on the deck beside us. We told him we were not acquainted with some of the passengers, and if we stood up whenever a European was passing we should get tired before we got to our destination. At this reply he became

[6] *An African Speaks for His People*, P. G. Mockerie, pp. 12–13.

very angry and began to rail against African societies, how they collect funds and organize themselves and become independent of the missionaries. Next morning when I found he refrained from speaking to me, I reminded him of the Biblical phrase, 'Let not the sun go down upon your anger.' From this time onwards we were friendly until we left the boat."[7]

To their dismay the two of them found that when they got to England the Joint Select Committee had refused to hear any more witnesses. As the only official African witnesses from Kenya were Government appointees, despite the fact that the European and Asian witnesses had been chosen by their own people, this was a hard blow. However, the memorandum which they had brought with them was presented to the Committee, although it was never published in the final official Blue Book. The memorandum, written in a crude but forceful style, was a passionate document listing Kikuyu grievances.

The authors, Kenyatta among them, began by stressing the difficulties which faced them in this attempt to present their complaints in the correct English manner, for people to whom Africans "are a species of living being which was hardly known to them about fifty years ago." The authors went on to add that their difficulties were aggravated by the fact that their organization was "not only gagged but crippled and tied by hands and feet, for we are not only denied the freedom of speech and press, but we are also forbidden from holding meetings and even collecting funds to enable us to make our voice reach the ears of the civilized world . . . Our honest efforts for making the truth known to the outside world and especially to the British people is construed as seditious and revolutionary while in

[7] *Ibid.*, pp. 15–16.

reality we are rendering a real service to the British people by acquainting them with the real feelings of the people whose destinies they have taken upon themselves to rule and control." From their point of view, the few material benefits of civilization which they had received were outweighed by the loss of land and personal liberty.

Although the Committee refused to see them officially, some of their English friends of the Union of Democratic Control arranged a meeting at the House of Commons at which they both spoke. Some members of the Joint Select Committee were present. An incident occurred after the meeting which Parmenas recorded.

"A young imperialist who was in the audience came to talk with me in the corridor of the House of Commons after the meeting. He wished that there had been a Kenya European to answer the questions which we raised at the meeting. In his conversation he was frank in telling me that social and political equality between Europeans and Africans were inconceivable. I asked him whether a man could be considered just who, having accepted the responsibility of a family, discriminated between his children, giving some good food and the others bad. His reply was that Africans should be taught on their own lines, and that he was disgusted when he saw Africans speaking in the House of Commons, which was a place for white men. We departed courteously. . . ."[8]

Soon afterwards the two men gave talks on East Africa at a Fabian Summer School at Farnham, near London. There they managed to corner the Under-Secretary of State for the Colonies in the then Labour Government and he gave them a promise that he would "look into the matter."

[8] *Ibid.*, p. 18.

However, the minority Government was on its last legs and soon resigned.

Presenting the Kikuyu case to one committee after another must have put a considerable strain on Jomo Kenyatta, whose English at this stage was by no means perfect. A strong sense of injustice had to be neatly wrapped up in suitable phraseology, and delivered to men who, while often sympathetic, had well-trained analytical minds and very little direct experience of personal indignities. And imaginative insight was at a discount in the European character at that time. Settling arguments by Blue Books rather than spears was an art it took some years to master.

Another committee which he attended in 1930 was one, consisting of Members of Parliament, appointed by the Government, to consider the emotional subject of female circumcision. In 1929 the decision by the Church of Scotland mission in Kenya to try to stamp out this custom brought the controversy to a head. A missionary was murdered, and many schools were first boycotted and then closed down. Female circumcision, although a physically crude practice, played a vital part in the life of a Kikuyu woman. It marked her entry into womanhood, and without it she felt lost and was often looked down on by her friends. No man at that time — except an occasional Christian — would marry an uncircumcised girl.

A missionary who was in Kikuyuland soon after this dispute told me of one "extremely attractive" girl who was the undisputed "belle" of the district. Her Christian parents told her that they would not allow her to be circumcised, as it was not Christian. Overnight she became utterly miserable, and two days later she was blind. She was taken to a doctor who, after the examination, told the missionary

that the blindness was entirely emotional and connected
with her anxiety over circumcision. He wisely recom-
mended that her parents should give her a free choice in
the matter, which they did, and her sight returned. The
missionary was criticized by her superiors for her act of
generosity in this incident, which illustrates the human
suffering which can so easily result from an ill-considered
imposition of theory on custom.

In true British fashion, a group of dignified M.P.s solemnly discussed this topic in the mock-Gothic calm of
the House of Commons, Jomo Kenyatta explaining to them
the full significance of the operation, and urging that this
custom should be allowed to die a natural death under the
impact of education. This argument was accepted, but the
harm was already done in one important respect.

In Kenya the controversy had two consequences. One
was that the closing down of some schools led to the demand for independent Kikuyu schools, later said by the
Government to have played a leading role in the spread of
Mau Mau. Another consequence of equal importance was
the blow that it gave to the tentative approval of many
Kikuyu for the Christian religion. The "People of God"
won many adherents as a result. Instead of the bond between black and white becoming stronger each year, a
kind of dreary suspicion had begun to set in. In the eyes of
many Africans, particularly those with some education, the
onetime "angels" were evolving into warders in an open
prison, some with good intentions and some without. As
far as the Europeans were concerned, the Africans within
their control were beginning to fall into one of two cate-
gories — the good ones, who smiled easily, were well intentioned, often inefficient and liable to mistake the soup
for the gravy, but who never answered back; and the bad

ones, usually with a mission education, who wore flashy European clothes, wanted jobs as clerks, thought they could do anything, and, because they often answered back, were therefore "cheeky." Prospero grew quite fond of his tame Ariel, but began to dislike intensely the Caliban whom his education was beginning to produce in ever increasing numbers. These "cheeky boys" were a warning by human nature that the "civilizing mission" could become a costly failure unless it could rise above the cautious selfishness of a limited liability company with an eye on the profits. The warning passed unheeded.

In London, at the source of power, Jomo Kenyatta continued his often lonely and always difficult task of influencing decisions before they were exported to Kenya as irrevocable orders. In 1932 he gave evidence before the Kenya Land Commission, usually referred to as the Carter Commission, after its chairman, Sir Morris Carter. This Commission will go down in history for its ability to recognize the trees but miss the wood. With meticulous care it went into the thousands of claims relating to often very small areas of land, and where it decided that land had been wrongfully alienated it awarded compensation. It decided that the Kikuyu had been illegally deprived of just over one hundred square miles and so made them an award of what it considered to be an equivalent area elsewhere — a solution which looked neat on the map, but which was of little use to the families concerned, who did not want to move many miles away to a new district.

The Commission saw that alienation of land for the use of settlers had "increased the density of the native population in the Kikuyu Reserve," and it saw that a couple of thousand white farmers had 10,000 square miles of farm and ranch land, of which only a small proportion was cultivated. Another 6,000 square miles were empty, waiting to be settled. But it acted like a man who mends a window while his house burns down. It made the White Highlands of the settlers into a virtually sacrosanct white reserve, settled the shape of the African areas, with a few bits added on here and there, and then announced that unless something was done quite soon there would be trouble.

There was no African on the Commission. The Africans were not permitted to get title deeds for their land, to buy land in the White Highlands, or to win any sort of guarantee that population needs would be taken into account in the future. Areas of Kikuyuland with over two hundred people to the square mile bordered on wide areas of rich farmland occupied by a few European farmers. Nothing lay between them but an Order in Council and the slowly eroding myth of white supremacy.

In London Jomo Kenyatta's indignation occasionally spilled over in his attempts to persuade friends and enemies that the cry of "more land" was not the whim of a spoilt child but a necessity of life. Later, he expressed his feelings about commissions more delicately, in a fable, which had an ominous twist at the end for anyone who cared to listen. Introducing it he writes:

The relation between the Gikuyu and the Europeans can well be illustrated by a Gikuyu story . . . Once upon a time an elephant made a friendship with a man. One day a heavy thunderstorm broke out, the elephant went to his friend, who had a little hut at the edge of the forest, and said to him: "My dear good man, will you please let me put my trunk inside your hut to keep it outside this torrential rain?" The man, seeing what situation his friend was in, replied: "My dear good elephant, my hut is very small, but there is room for your trunk and myself. Please put your trunk in gently." The elephant thanked his friend, saying: "You have done me a good deed and one day I shall return your kindness." But what followed? As soon as the elephant put his trunk inside the hut, slowly he pushed his head inside, and finally flung the man out in the rain, and then lay down comfortably inside his friend's hut, saying: "My dear good friend, your skin is harder than mine, and as there is not enough room for both of us, you can afford to remain in the rain while I am protecting my delicate skin from the hailstorm."

The man, seeing what his friend had done to him, started to grumble, the animals in the nearby forest heard the noise and came to see what was the matter. All stood around listening to the heated argument between the man and his friend the elephant. In this turmoil the lion came along roaring, and said in a loud voice: "Don't you all know that I am the King of the Jungle! How dare anyone disturb the peace of my kingdom?" On hearing this the elephant, who was one of the high ministers in the jungle kingdom, replied in a soothing voice, and said: "My Lord, there is no disturbance of the peace in your kingdom. I have only been having a little discussion with my friend here as to the possession of this little hut which your lordship sees me occupying." The lion, who wanted to have "peace and tranquility" in his kingdom, replied in a noble voice, saying: "I command my ministers to appoint a Commission of Enquiry to go thoroughly into this matter and report accordingly." He then turned to the man and said: "You have done well by establishing friendship with my people, especially with the elephant who is one of my honourable ministers of state. Do not grumble any more, your hut is not lost to you. Wait until the sitting of my Imperial Commission, and there you will be given plenty of opportunity to state your case. I am sure you will be pleased with the findings of the commission." The man was very pleased by these sweet words from the King of the Jungle, and innocently waited for his opportunity, in the belief that naturally the hut would be returned to him.

The elephant, obeying the command of his master, got busy with other ministers to appoint the Commission of Enquiry. The following elders of the jungle were appointed to sit on the commission: (1) Mr. Rhinoceros; (2) Mr. Buffalo; (3) Mr. Alligator; (4) The Rt. Hon. Mr. Fox to act as chairman; and (5) Mr. Leopard to act as Secretary to the commission. On seeing the personnel, the man protested and asked if it was not necessary to include in this commission a member from his side. But he was told that it was impossible, since no one from his side was well enough educated to understand the intricacy of jungle law. Further, that there was nothing to fear, for the members of the commission were all men of repute for their impartiality in justice, and as they were gentlemen chosen by God to look after the interests of races less adequately endowed with teeth and claws, he might rest assured that they would investigate the matter with the greatest care and report impartially.

The commission sat to take the evidence. The Rt. Hon. Mr. Elephant was first called. He came along with a superior air, brushing his tusks with a sapling which Mrs. Elephant had provided, and in an authoritative voice said: "Gentlemen of the Jungle, there is no need for me to waste your valuable time in relating a story which I am sure you all know. I have always regarded it as my duty to protect the interests of my friends, and this appears to have caused the misunderstandings between myself and my friend here. He invited me to save his hut from being blown away by a hurricane. As the hurricane had gained access owing to the unoccupied space in the hut, I considered it necessary, in my friend's own interests, to turn the undeveloped space to a more economic use by sitting in it myself; a duty which any of you would undoubtedly have performed with equal readiness in similar circumstances."

After hearing the Rt. Hon. Mr. Elephant's conclusive evidence, the commission called Mr. Hyena and other elders of the jungle, who all supported what Mr. Elephant had said. They then called the man who began to give his

own account of the dispute. But the commission cut him
short, saying: "My good man, please confine yourself to
relevant issues. We have already heard the circumstances
from various unbiased sources; all we wish you to tell us
is whether the undeveloped space in your hut was occupied by anyone else before Mr. Elephant assumed his
position?" The man began to say: "No, but — ." But at this
point the commission declared that they had heard sufficient evidence from both sides and retired to consider their
decision. After enjoying a delicious meal at the expense of
the Rt. Hon. Mr. Elephant, they reached their verdict,
called the man, and declared as follows: "In our opinion
this dispute has arisen through a regrettable misunder-
standing due to the backwardness of your ideas. We consider that Mr. Elephant has fulfilled his sacred duty of
protecting your interests. As it is clearly for your good that
the space should be put to its most economic use, and as
you yourself have not yet reached the stage of expansion
which would enable you to fulfill it, we consider it necessary to arrange a compromise to suit both parties. Mr.
Elephant shall continue his occupation of your hut, but we
give you permission to look for a site where you can build
another hut more suited to your needs, and we will see
that you are well protected."

The man, having no alternative, and fearing that his
refusal might expose him to the teeth and claws of members of the commission, did as they suggested. But no
sooner had he built another hut than Mr. Rhinoceros
charged in with his horn lowered and ordered the man to
quit. A Royal Commission was again appointed to look
into the matter, and the same finding was given. This
procedure was repeated until Mr. Buffalo, Mr. Leopard,
Mr. Hyena, and the rest were all accommodated with new
huts. Then the man decided that he must adopt an effective
method of protection, since Commissions of Enquiry did
not seem to be of any use to him. He sat down and said:
"Ng'enda thi ndagaga motegi," which literally means
"There is nothing that treads on the earth that cannot be

trapped," or in other words, "You can fool people for a time, but not for ever."

Early one morning, when the huts already occupied by the jungle lords were all beginning to decay and fall to pieces, he went out and built a bigger and better hut a little distance away. No sooner had Mr. Rhinoceros seen it than he came rushing in, only to find that Mr. Elephant was already inside, sound asleep. Mr. Leopard next came in at the window, Mr. Lion, Mr. Fox, and Mr. Buffalo entered the doors, while Mr. Hyena howled for a place in the shade and Mr. Alligator basked on the roof. Presently they all began disputing about their rights and penetration, and from disputing they came to fighting, and while they were all embroiled together the man set the hut on fire and burnt it to the ground, jungle lords and all. Then he went home, saying: "Peace is costly, but it's worth the expense," and lived happily ever after.[9]

[9] *Facing Mount Kenya*, p. 47.

CHAPTER FIVE

A STARTLING NEW WORLD

A PERSON who knew Jomo Kenyatta well during his early years in England points out that, behind an intermittent political life, appearing before various commissions on East African affairs, he lived in a state of constant tension. Nairobi, for all its veneer of European mechanics, was physically very close to traditional Africa, and Africans who worked there, such as Kenyatta, kept in frequent touch with their tribal society. In London he had only his naturally strong vitality, and some friends, to help him make the thousand and one adjustments which his new life demanded of him. Brought up first as a member of a tightly knit society, in which individual personality was suppressed to ensure maximum social unity, he now found himself in an almost exactly opposite situation. In the England of those days, and particularly in the large towns, it was often a case of each man for himself and the devil take the hindmost. Private enterprise and the competitive spirit were the guiding stars, and the "hindmost" had to rely mainly on spasmodic human kindness and a few poor welfare societies.

Kenyatta was lucky to find some good friends, some of whom were quite influential. During the whole of his sixteen-year stay in England he was never without some friends and acquaintances. Many of these were connected with left-wing political circles and were interested in

colonial problems; the sort of people whom the Kenya
settlers regarded as "misinformed liberals." Among them
was the brother of Dr. Norman Leys, who had written
some highly critical comments on British rule in Kenya
after he had retired from working there. Mr. Leys, who
taught at a Quaker college in Birmingham, did all he could
to help Kenyatta educationally, and welcomed him into his
home. Others, who were glad of the opportunity of meeting
a representative from one of the colonies whose cause they
could only champion in the abstract, included the late
Lady Cynthia Asquith, many members of the Quaker
Friends' Council for International Service, and Labour
party members. He was given hospitality by such well-
known Labour leaders as Ramsay MacDonald and Sidney
and Beatrice Webb. However, much of this hospitality,
though genuinely well intentioned, tended to emphasize
his essential loneliness at this period. Owing to a disparity
of personal backgrounds, these early friendships had nec-
essarily to remain at fingertip distance.

In the autumn of 1931 Kenyatta moved to Birmingham.
He lived in the Quaker college where Mr. Leys taught, at
Woodbrooke, Selly Oak. He had been advised to go there
by those friends of his first visit to England, the McGregor
Rosses and Freer Andrews. This move, like his earlier brief
journey to Russia, was an opportunity for Kenyatta to
study Western ideas at first hand. His friends hoped that
the friendly atmosphere of the college would help him
adjust to the English way of life.

When he arrived at Woodbrooke his English was far
from perfect, but at the end of two terms he passed a
certificate in English composition. Even so he sometimes
had difficulty in expressing himself, and the Woodbrooke
log records that he once asked a student: "Have you been

baptised?" To which the facetious reply was offered: "Oh yes, baptised once and vaccinated three times." Puzzled, Kenyatta asked: "All in the same church?" and then, after a flash of enlightenment, "Oh, fascinated! I have been fascinated only once."

His fellow students recall him as normally rather quiet and reticent, but sometimes popular and even gay when the occasion arose. A nickname which was bestowed on him by the children of a Quaker household with which he had spent Christmas was taken up by the students, and he was thereafter known by them as "Uncle Ken." He was, in fact, about ten years older than most of the students, although this does not seem to have inhibited him from taking part in many of the social functions. On these occasions he sometimes entertained his friends with his exuberant singing and dancing.

One man who knew him at this time described Jomo Kenyatta's manner as "gentle," and said that this won him a wide response from those whom he met. Another says that he was "quiet and unassuming and had pleasant manners." Perhaps this may have been one reason why he was an undoubted success with the women students, who spoilt him by doing his mending for him and knitting him pullovers. As a photo taken of him at about this time shows, he was handsome, well made, and had an engaging smile.

Apart from his English studies he showed a particular interest in the lectures on international and social affairs, and at one of these he spoke eloquently about the troubles of his tribe. Its theme was recorded, equally eloquently, by a member of the same class:

We have a good man here from Kenya,
The settlers don't know that he's been here.

When I asked, "Are they kind?"
He replied, "Yes — you'll find
They're as kind as the Turks in Armenia."

Although he was the only African at Woodbrooke, he did
not allow himself to become isolated in Birmingham. He
frequently left his studies for a day or two to attend meetings and give lectures on Kenya. One incident in particular
aroused his anger, the Scottsboro case in the U.S.A., and
he took an active part in organizing public protests in
England.

Partly perhaps because social and political issues occupied such a dominant place in English thinking at that
time, Jomo Kenyatta seems to have paid little attention to
European religious beliefs. A former missionary says that
he kept in "desultory touch" with the headquarters of the
Church Missionary Society in London. He adds that Kenyatta came to England with the record of a practising
Christian which "partly due to his lack of finance, and
partly to his determination to 'get on,' degenerated into a
nominal Christianity, retained as a means of widening his
circle of acquaintances." Although he had such close contact with a number of Quakers there is no evidence that
he took more than a critical and friendly interest in Quaker-
ism. Occasionally he attended their religious meetings, but
he is not thought to have spoken at any of them.

Kenyatta, in other words, was pursuing a line which was
being followed by millions of others all over the Western
world — nominal Christianity. Unlike religion in Kikuyuland, which enclosed every aspect of tribal life, European
religion had become divorced over the years from what
became known as the secular world. As politics, economics,
and science were generally associated with the secular
world, and these appeared to include all the most pressing

problems of the time, most Europeans either consciously
or unconsciously followed Mammon, while retaining a
nominal link with the God of their fathers, now little more
than a distant glow on the mental horizon.

Jomo Kenyatta, however, was far from insensitive to
spiritual realities. He appreciated the atmosphere of his
Quaker college, as the following account of it shows, which
he wrote at the time:

When first I arrived at this place I heard a great deal
about the "Spirit of Woodbrooke," and those who would
pull my leg told me that it was a kind of white and yellow
mixture served at most meals. I quickly learned, however,
that there was much more in the "Spirit of Woodbrooke"
than ever came out of a basin of custard, and that the stuff
so nicknamed was not the real adhesive which binds
Woodbrookers together during their time at Selly Oak, and
in the larger world outside.

He who stays but for one meal at Woodbrooke may
perchance catch no more of the Spirit than is served out
to him on his plate, but dull would he be of soul who could
abide for many hours within these portals without awakening to the more subtle essence which makes us all one
family in our work and play.

To call the custard, which nourishes the body and fits
us for our work, the "Spirit of Woodbrooke" is excellent as
a joke, but served alone without the true Spirit of Woodbrooke it would be of little avail, for it is this greater Spirit
which lends zest and purpose to all our activities.

What then is the real Spirit of Woodbrooke? It is the
Spirit which forces men and women to realize their mu-
tual responsibility in life; it teaches them to think of
others, and not to take thought alone for their own comfort, pleasure or salvation. This Spirit I hold must grow to
pervade all classes of the community, irrespective of rank
or station, colour or race. It is a Spirit that will raise men
by its unselfishness, will redeem them by its personal ap-

peal, will broaden their views, so that where now they see but creed and dogma, they will see Truth. It will indeed teach us that we, the children of humanity, being brothers and sisters, must serve one another in the love of all mankind, to the benefit of all life, and to the advancement and ultimate perfection of those who are yet to come.

Surely the Spirit of Woodbrooke teaches us patience in trial, resignation in affliction, humbleness in success, and virtue in whatever position in life it has pleased God to place us. Above all, the Spirit of Woodbrooke is the Spirit of True Fellowship.

This passage is a good indication of the route by which Kenyatta was introduced both to the English language and to English culture. It might well be an extract from a sensible but rather heavy sermon, which is not in the least surprising considering that Kenyatta's first English lessons were at the hands of a Scottish mission. Whatever their other admirable characteristics the Scots in general, and the Scottish church in particular, are not noted for lightness of touch. Religion in England itself was encased in such an antique terminology that even the Quakers, who did their best to express their religious convictions in comprehensive language, were often driven back on the old forms for want of anything better.

Judging by later examples of Kenyatta's writing, it is unlikely that his emotional and exuberant spirit felt very much at ease within these stiff phrases. As for the sentiments themselves, they show to what an extent Kenyatta had himself absorbed the Spirit of Woodbrooke, if not its religious externals.

When he left the college Kenyatta was running short of money; a fairly frequent occurrence during his stay in Europe. Sometimes it was the K.C.A. in Kenya which rescued him and sometimes it was his English friends. On this occasion it was the Quaker family with whom he had spent Christmas who bailed him out. In his tribal society it was taken for granted that any member of the tribe was entitled to help by the others. This was due as much to self-interest as generosity, because no man in the tribe could be happy unless it was a unified whole. This may help to explain what to a European seems to be the somewhat lax way many Africans handle money matters. Kenyatta was not always an exception and at one stage had run up a debt with a poor but indulgent landlady who could not afford to be kept waiting for payment of the sum. Another friend lent him 10 pounds at this time. McGregor Ross was so upset over Kenyatta's financial position, according to this friend, that he tried to get him to return to Kenya, without success.

That Jomo Kenyatta found it a hard task to anchor himself firmly in this new society is indicated by one of his fellow students, who says:

"In many ways he was less mature than most of the young Quakers of twenty. He was like a young schoolboy let loose in a startling new world where everything was exciting. He just did not seem to know how to use these experiences; the friendships, the hospitality, the comfortable life at Woodbrooke. He was of course unique and, in consequence, was in great demand, particularly by those deeply interested in social justice and the colour problem . . . In many respects he was feted too much: people lost their sense of proportion in those days when there was just one African about."

His two short visits to Russia must have further confused Jomo Kenyatta as to his own value in the eyes of the Europeans he had met. For those who disliked colonialism on principle Kenyatta was a living symbol of oppression.

For those who supported it as a civilizing influence he
was an object of paternalist affection. In either case it was
most unlikely that his sympathizers would have more than
the haziest ideas of the details of his background in Kenya.
As a living symbol of one of Europe's most pressing historical and psychological problems Jomo Kenyatta had a
hard job trying to win recognition for his personality in its
own right.

His first visit to Russia had caused great interest and
excitement among his Quaker friends at Woodbrooke. In
1933 he returned for another short visit of three months,
and, according to the Corfield Report, unconfirmed elsewhere, he attended an institution with the Machiavellian
name of the Lenin School of Subversion.[1] Although Kenyatta was a member of the Communist Party in Britain
during the early thirties it is probable that he regarded
Communism as yet another interesting aspect of Western
civilization with which he had to come to terms. He no
more became a lasting Communist than he became a con-
vinced Quaker, although he found something to admire
in both.

One impression of this second visit which did stick in
his mind was the progress being made by the once nomadic Yakuts, a people in East Russia who had been
classed by the Czars as a "backward race." Paul Robeson,
the famous American Negro singer, shared a flat with Kenyatta at this time near Charing Cross in London, and they
often discussed Russia. Paul Robeson recalls of his friend:
"He had been struck by the resemblance between the
tribal life of the Yakuts and his own people in East Africa.
What would happen to a people like the Yakuts now that
they had been freed from colonial oppression and were

[1] Corfield Report, p. 43.

part of the construction of a socialist society?"[2] Paul Robeson had the chance to find out a year or so later and
thought they were "leaping ahead" towards a modern
economy.

Sharing the same flat with Paul Robeson and Kenyatta
was Peter Abrahams, the West Indian writer. As non-
Europeans they were an unusually articulate fragment of
that huge part of the world's population which was searching for its own identity, the right to be itself and become
something more than trainees of the powerful culture built
up in Europe. Disillusioned by the position accorded to
Negroes in his homeland, the United States, Paul Robeson
came to London, where he "felt at home," and began to
take an interest in Africa and its own problems. He, like the
others, became increasingly depressed by the currently
popular theory of "gradualism," whereby the colonial powers estimated that, as they themselves had spent about a
thousand years becoming civilized, it would require about
the same time for the colonies to become ripe for independence. It never seems to have occurred to them that,
as with the inefficient steam engine, a vast proportion of
their ancestors' energy had been misdirected. Impatience
with "gradualism" is summed up perfectly in an old Negro
slave song:

> *My old master promised me*
> *When he died he'd set me free,*
> *He lived so long that his head got bald*
> *And he gave up the notion of dying at all.*[3]

But beneath the warmhearted sentimental resignation of
the American Negro, Paul Robeson possessed the seeds of

[2] *Here I Stand*, Paul Robeson, p. 43.

[3] *Ibid.*, p. 83.

that dynamic vitality which had driven another Negro leader, Toussaint L'Ouverture, whom he greatly admired. The Spirit of Woodbrooke must have had to fight for its life in Kenyatta when he heard Paul Robeson quote the speech by Toussaint L'Ouverture to his Haitian rebels: "My children, France comes to make us slaves. God gave us liberty; France has no right to take it away. Burn the cities, destroy the harvest, tear up the roads with cannon, poison the wells, show the white man the hell he comes to make!" It required 30,000 of Napoleon's soldiers to crush him.

Paul Robeson acknowledges how much he learnt about African culture from Kenyatta, and in his turn he taught Kenyatta many of the American Negro songs which he used later to sing to his son Peter.

It was not only the nationalist movements of the past which fired the imagination of Kenyatta and many of his contemporaries but also such incidents as the Italian invasion of Ethiopia, then almost the only independent African country. From 1934 onwards this shabby event did much to stimulate African nationalism. Jomo Kenyatta became Honorary Secretary of the International African Friends of Abyssinia Society, with offices in London. Among those on his executive committee were Mohammed Said, of Somaliland; Dr. J. D. Danquah of what was then the Gold Coast; and a Negro actor, John Payne.

From the time of his return from Russia in 1933 until 1936, Jomo Kenyatta worked in the department of African phonetics at University College, London, as an "informant." His job was to assist the senior lecturer in phonetics on a study of the tones and phonetics of the Kikuyu language. He also taught Kikuyu in another part of the University of London, the School of Oriental and African languages.

In 1936 he went to the London School of Economics to take the Diploma in Anthropology under Professor Malinowski. The course was at postgraduate level, designed for students who, although they did not hold degrees, had a "special acquaintance with native life." Kenyatta's fees were paid by an organization of impeccable reputation in the academic world, now known as the International African Institute. The chairman of its executive council at that time was that grand old man of honest imperialism, Lord Lugard. During his year at the London School of Economics, Kenyatta became very friendly with Prince Peter of Denmark, a fellow-anthropologist, and on leaving the school, he accepted an invitation from the Prince to visit Denmark. A friend says that he was particularly impressed by the Danes' co-operative agricultural colleges, and felt strongly that this was an idea worth trying out among the Kikuyu in Kenya.

The course was a magnificent opportunity for Kenyatta and, characteristically, he seized it with both hands. Almost more than politics, anthropology could lead towards a cultural redemption of the Kikuyu people, and here Kenyatta had the chance to meet some of the world's leading anthropologists. Raymond Firth, now Professor of Anthropology at the University of London, remembers that his three seminar papers were "original, thoughtful, and showed an excellent mastery of anthropology for a student new to the subject." His studies added a new dimension to his understanding of the strengths and weaknesses of his people, as judged from a Western standpoint. The papers which impressed his teachers dealt with Kikuyu customs — land tenure, the structure of authority, religion and magic.

His strong convictions on these topics now found the

relief of an outlet through the medium of more disciplined thought-forms. One member of the seminar on magic says that he remembers wondering whether Kenyatta, although he had dealt with the topic in anthropological terms, did not feel that there was some intrinsic value in Kikuyu magic. The effect of white rule provoked some strong opinions from him but he never let them degenerate into a list of inflammatory grievances. According to Professor Firth, he was respected by the other students and had an air of *gravitas* about him. One fellow-student, a well-known writer on Kenya, was less impressed. She thought that, though able, self-confident, and eloquent, he was "clearly ambitious and an intriguer, and always struck me personally as a rather sinister personality, but I'm afraid I can't say exactly why . . ."

Professor Malinowski, one of the leading figures in the anthropological world, thought so highly of Kenyatta's efforts that he encouraged him to expand his work into a book, to which he himself wrote the preface. This book, *Facing Mount Kenya*, marked Kenyatta's final initiation into the intellectual world of Europe. He no longer had to express his buoyant African nature theatrically by posing for photographs in tribal skins — handsome, but faintly ridiculous, holding a spear. He could now tackle the "civilizing mission" on its own ground, with the force of disciplined ideas, made dynamic by strong feeling.

CHAPTER SIX

RABBIT TURNED POACHER

"I've written it and read it, written and read it until it doesn't make sense to me any longer; I want someone to arrange the chapters in their proper order." This appeal, familiar to anyone who has been bemused by his own writing, was addressed by Jomo Kenyatta to his friend, Dinah Stock, after he had completed the manuscript of *Facing Mount Kenya.* She did as she was asked and the book was published in 1938, being favourably received in England. When it was reprinted in 1953, at the height of the Mau Mau rebellion, that tireless collector of information on Africa, Lord Hailey, described it as "still the best book on the Kikuyu."

Facing Mount Kenya is almost as revealing of its author as it is of the Kikuyu tribe. Most anthropologists chase happily after their chosen people with notebooks at the ready and with boundless enthusiasm and patience, but when the result is in print it can be depressing. The passions and customs of living men and women lie like dead butterflies between dry pages, their life replaced by a bleak skeleton of clans, sub-clans, totemism, and matrilineal diagrams. For Jomo Kenyatta *Facing Mount Kenya* was much more than just anthropology. It was a justification, in modern dress, of the traditional way of life of his tribe, and indirectly of himself. Like the eddies of white steam which rise from cracks in the otherwise extinct crater

of Longonot, on the border of Kikuyuland, personal emotion sometimes disturbs the attempted calm of this survey.
Kenyatta had earned for himself in England personal
friendship and recognition, but it seems clear from his
writing that he knew very well, and felt strongly, that the
African people as a whole were still far from winning such
recognition from the rest of the world. The pages of *Facing
Mount Kenya* reveal how deeply he felt himself to be
part of the Kikuyu heritage. He would never find any real
peace within himself until his past, his tribe, and his present self could be linked to create a new whole.

The book is dedicated to "Muigoi and Wamboi and all
the dispossessed youth of Africa: for perpetuation and
communion with ancestral spirits through the fight for
African Freedom, and in the firm faith that the dead, the
living, and the unborn will unite to rebuild the destroyed
shrines." In his Introduction Professor Malinowski writes
sombrely and with strong feeling of the crumbling Europe
in which the book was written; a Europe which had
emerged from one brutal war only to stagger blindly
towards the next; and where man, despite his ever increasing knowledge, was a prey to "bluff, impudence, and
aggression." He gave a warning which, had it been heeded,
would have saved Africa from many of its later setbacks.

"The educated, intellectual minority of Africans," he
wrote, "usually dismissed as 'agitators,' are rapidly becoming a force. They are catalysing an African public opinion
even among the raw tribesmen. A great deal will depend
on whether this minority of 'agitators' will be made to keep
a balanced and moderate view of economic, social and
political issues, or whether by ignoring them and treating
them with contempt we drive them into the open arms of
world-wide Bolshevism. For on this will depend the gen-

eral drift of African opinion from one end of the Dark Continent to the other." Professor Malinowski considered that not only was *Facing Mount Kenya* "an invaluable document in the principles underlying culture-contact and change," but also, as an example of the "new outlook of a progressive African," "a pioneering achievement of outstanding merit."

Facing Mount Kenya has been described by some people as a sentimental glorification of his tribe as a race of "Black Siegfrieds," always chivalrous and brave. It is true that there is no word of criticism of the Kikuyu tribe and its customs, but then an anthropological study is supposed to be an exposition of human society rather than an evaluation of it. Criticism, if it is fair, is better aimed at the occasional derogatory asides about the behaviour of Kenya Europeans. But for the person interested in Kenyatta's personal evolution it is these asides which provide much of the book's interest.

In his Preface, Kenyatta at once joins battle with his many unseen opponents who claim a monopoly of interpreting the African mind, and he admits without apology that for these people he is now "a rabbit turned poacher." After expressing his thanks to all those who helped him he tosses a debonair wave at his enemies. "I owe thanks also to my enemies, for the stimulating discouragement which has kept up my spirits to persist in the task. Long life and health to them to go on with the good work!" And after a decorous bow to the "very considerable restraint" under which he has tried to keep his "sense of political grievances" he quickly returns to the fray. "But the African is not blind. He can recognize these pretenders to philanthropy, and in various parts of the continent he is waking up to the realisation that a running river cannot be dammed for ever without breaking its bounds. His power of expression has been hampered, but it is breaking through, and will very soon sweep away the patronage and repression which surround him."

In the section on land, Kenyatta writes how, "misled by European cant, the Gikuyu thought that the Europeans with their caravans did not mean any harm and befriended them . . . The Gikuyu looked upon them as wanderers (*orori*, or *athongo*) who had deserted from their homes and were lonely and in need of friends . . . The Gikuyu, in their natural generosity and hospitality, welcomed the wanderers and felt pity for them . . . The Europeans were treated in this way in the belief that one day they would get tired of wandering and finally return to their own country . . . These early Empire builders, knowing what they were after, played on the ignorance and sincere hospitable nature of the people."[1] There is an air of slightly unreal injured innocence about Kenyatta's writing on this point, but there is no doubt that much of it is justified historically, and that few of the early Europeans in Kenya were the "right men" advocated by Lugard.

In view of later accusations that Kenyatta was implacably opposed to Government efforts to develop the Kikuyu reserve, it is interesting to note his awareness at this time of the need to improve the economic capacity of his tribe. "From the economic point of view," he writes, "the present breed of cattle reared by the Gikuyu is very poor, and it would be a great advancement if the Government could help the people to secure a few good bulls for breeding, and gradually replace the inferior types of cattle with better ones."

The zoo-like restrictions on "native movement" in Kenya

[1] *Facing Mount Kenya*, pp. 44–45.

at that time also came in for some sharp criticism. "The friendly relation between the Gikuyu and the Wakamba," he writes, "is still the same, except that free visiting is now prohibited, and only those who have a special pass from the British Government can visit either Gikuyu or Wakamba country or other tribes."[2] The Hut Tax was denounced. "Nowadays," he writes, "the system of having two huts for a man with only one wife is dying out, owing to the heavy burden of hut taxes imposed on the people . . . The result has been congestion, whole families being crowded in one hut. . . ."[3]

In an account of Kikuyu traditional weapons a note of sarcasm creeps in: "It is worth our while here to note that the Kenya Government has put a ban on the Africans carrying dangerous weapons, namely, spears, swords, and bows and arrows. At the same time the Europeans move freely in town and in country carrying all sorts of fire-arms. The Africans, seeing these, marvel at the European conception of 'dangerous weapons.' "[4]

But the fate of Kikuyu weapons and the quality of their cows clearly did not arouse the same interest or emotion in Kenyatta as did the subject of education. His treatment of Kikuyu education and its carefully phased introduction of the young boy or girl into tribal society gives the reader an insight into the confusion which inevitably followed the sudden imposition of Western academic methods. The whole of Kenyatta's analysis is an eloquent plea that European educationalists should make a sympathetic study of tribal ways before attempting to change them to fit new conditions. It is in no sense a denunciation of change as such.

Kenyatta saw very clearly that the root difference be-

[2] *Ibid.*, p. 69.   [3] *Ibid.*, p. 77.   [4] *Ibid.*, p. 86.

tween African and Western education lay in the position accorded to the individual. In the tribal system the individual was taught how to come to terms, not with himself, but with society. The Western pattern, while probably not as concerned with individual development as sometimes assumed, laid much emphasis in principle on the training of character. Except in the better schools, however, academic knowledge and examinations often took pride of place and it was left to the gods as to whether the child acquired the strength of character which alone made his knowledge worth while. This fundamental weakness became quickly apparent in Africa and Kenyatta recognized, as did many missionary teachers, that knowledge was a feeble thing when not related to the environment in which it was taught.

"While the Westerner asserts," writes Kenyatta, "that character formation is the chief thing, he forgets that character is formed primarily through relations with other people, and that there is really no other way in which it can grow. Europeans assume that, given the right knowledge and ideas, personal relations can be left largely to take care of themselves, and this is perhaps the most fundamental difference in outlook between Africans and Europeans."[5] He goes on to suggest that Western education, if it is to succeed, must be firmly related to the strong social ties which hold the tribe together. "In the past," he writes, "there has been too much of 'civilising and uplifting poor savages' . . . The European should realize that there is something to learn from the African and a great deal about him to understand, and that the burden could be made easier if a policy of 'give and take' could be adopted . . . By ignoring the African's point of view, and

[5] *Ibid.*, p. 121.

by insisting that pupils should adopt the European methods, whether the technique fits in with their mode of life or not, the teacher creates conflicts of ideas in the mental outlook of his pupils. . . ."[6]

Kenyatta suggests that if an educationalist could acquire a real understanding of African social structure he could "adopt a practical theory and method to suit the situation, and to satisfy the African aspiration, so that education, instead of creating confusion, might help to promote progress, and at the same time to preserve all that is best in the traditions of the African people and assist them to create a new culture which, though its roots are still in the soil, is yet modified to meet the pressure of modern conditions."[7] He concludes by taking the wind out of the sails of those people, and there are thousands extant, who claim to "know the African."

"While a European can learn something of the externals of African life, its system of kinship and classification, its peculiar arts and picturesque ceremonial, he may still have not yet reached the heart of the problem . . . With his preconceived ideas, mingled with prejudices, he fails to achieve a more sympathetic and imaginative knowledge, a more human and inward appreciation of the living people, the pupils he teaches, the people he meets on the roads and watches in the gardens. In a word, he fails to understand the African with his instinctive tendencies (no doubt very like his own), but trained from his earliest days to habitual ideas, inhibitions and forms of self-expression which have been handed down from one generation to another and which are foreign, if not absurd, to the European in Africa."

But Kenyatta's thoughtful ideas made no great impact on

[6] *Ibid.*, pp. 124–26. [7] *Ibid.*, p. 128.

the educational field in Kenya, though they were well received by friends in England. Ironically enough, the main reason why, with some exceptions, the European missionary teacher could not follow this advice was that he had been taught too little of that rare and valuable thing in Western education, a self-reliance which generates the good manners needed to approach foreign customs with sympathy. The result was that he took his cue from England, and England was fundamentally as uninterested in Kenya's local culture as Europe was in Africa's. Thanks to a suicidal blindness towards the source of its own civilizing genius, Europe and Western civilization were edging feebly towards another major breakdown in human relations and the Second World War. Politically and socially, if not individually, the white puppets on the Kenya stage continued to dance to the tune of Whitehall or of Victorian memories, but Africa itself was still the silent continent.

In his discussion of the traditional system of government Kenyatta claims that the old Kikuyu forms of government, before the arrival of the British, were based on "true democratic principles." This assertion must have caused some raised eyebrows amongst those who thought that Africans had emerged from some ghastly form of anarchic hooliganism. But it is a fact that by its system of government through councils of elders, who could maintain their authority only by the consent of the other adults, the Kikuyu tribe, like many others, had evolved a simple form of democracy. Kenyatta quotes the tribal legend which tells of the bad old days when there was a system of kingship. One king had proved unbearably despotic and had been dethroned by the young warriors, after which power became vested in the elders.

To emphasize this point, perhaps with a mischievous smile, Kenyatta quotes Aristotle:

"It seems probable that the reason why kingly government was the rule in early times is that it was rare to find persons of extremely eminent virtue . . . In process of time, however, there came to be a number of persons equally virtuous, and then they no longer submitted to kingly rule, but sought to establish a sort of commune or constitutional government. From Oligarchies they passed in the first instance to Tyrannies and from Tyrannies again to democracy."[8] Kenyatta explains that the appointment of chiefs by the British had been most unwise, because it was an artificial imposition. "The Gikuyu know perfectly well that these chiefs are appointed to represent a particular interest, namely, the interest of the British Government, and as such they cannot expect popularity from the people whom they help to oppress and exploit."[9]

Anger blazes momentarily from the pages as Kenyatta compares the fine pretensions of the civilizing mission with the actual consequences. He quotes the famous Devonshire White Paper on Kenya of 1923 which declared: "It is the mission of Great Britain to work continuously for the training and education of the Africans towards a higher intellectual, moral, and economic level than that which they had reached when the Crown assumed the responsibility for the administration of this territory." And he goes on to say bitterly:

"It is beyond our comprehension to see how a people can reach a so-called 'higher level' while they are denied the most elementary rights of self-expression, freedom of

[8] *The Politics of Aristotle*, Book 3, p. 151.

[9] *Facing Mount Kenya*, p. 196.

speech, the right to form social organizations to improve their condition, and above all, the right to move freely in their own country . . . Instead of advancing 'towards a higher intellectual, moral, and economic level,' the African has been reduced to a state of serfdom; his initiative in social, economic and political structure has been denied, his spirit of manhood has been killed and he has been subjected to the most inferior position in human society. If he dares to express his opinion on any point, other than that which is dictated to him, he is shouted at and black-listed as an 'agitator.' The tribal democratic institutions which were the boast of the country, and the proof of tribal good sense, have been suppressed. Oppressive laws and ordinances, which alone engross the monopoly of thought, of will, and of judgment, have been imposed on the African people. . . . In our opinion, the African can only advance to a 'higher level' if he is free to express himself, to organize economically, politically, and socially, and to take part in the government of his own country. In this way he will be able to develop his creative mind, initiative, and personality, which hitherto have been hindered by the multiplicity of incomprehensible laws and ordinances."[10]

This eloquent outburst is the language of nationalism in any part of the world, and represents the feelings of men fighting to win a new sense of adulthood in a new world and against an alien power. Its exaggerations are the exaggerations of strong emotion, but of essentially just emotion. History is littered with warnings about the folly of ignoring this human need, and Kenya was destined to provide yet another crop of gravestones as silent witness to human stupidity.

The abolishing of tribal warfare is touched on as another

[10] *Ibid.*, pp. 197–98.

example of unjustified European self-praise. Kenyatta scathingly compares the periodic raids after cattle with the wholesale slaughter of men in the Great War. For those settlers who talk glibly of the way the Masai used to terrorize the Kikuyu, he cites the case of his own grandmother who was a Masai and the frequent trading visits between the tribes. Kenyatta summarizes briefly:

"In the old order of the African society, with all the evils that are said to be connected with it, a man was a man, and as such he had the rights of a man and liberty to exercise his will and thought in a direction which suited his purposes as well as those of his fellow-men; but today an African, no matter what his station in life, is like a horse which moves only in the direction in which the rider pulls the rein."[11]

In his description of Kikuyu religious beliefs Kenyatta returns again to the theme of disunity resulting from European colonization. "The loss of the tribal unity is perhaps exemplified in the fact that formerly all the Gikuyu, with no exceptions whatever, believed in Mwene-Nyaga. It was a religion of tribal unity and helped to consolidate tribal organisation, both spiritually and materially. Now part of the people are Christians, Moslems, or merely 'detribalised,' having no religion at all."[12]

The missionaries are blamed for having come to Africa believing that the African was "a clean slate on which anything could be written." Kenyatta accuses the Europeans of believing that anyone could deal with "natives," so that, as a consequence, those who came to Kenya were often without proper qualifications for their job.

He attributes the growth of the new religious movements which attempted to find some common ground be-

[11] *Ibid.*, pp. 212–13.   [12] *Ibid.*, p. 251.

tween tribal and Christian (and sometimes Moslem) beliefs, to the European assumption of religious superiority. "The Europeans based their assumption on the conviction that everything that the African did or thought was evil. The missionaries endeavoured to rescue the depraved souls of the Africans from the 'eternal fire'; they set out to uproot the African, body and soul, from his old customs and beliefs, put him in a class by himself, with all his tribal traditions shattered and his institutions trampled upon."[13] The activities of some of these local religious movements will be referred to later, as they became an important factor in political developments.

In his Conclusion Kenyatta lists the main "progressive ideas" among the Europeans as material prosperity, medicine, hygiene, and literacy, but complains that they have brought very little of each to Africa. "If Africans were left in peace on their own lands, Europeans would have to offer them the benefits of white civilisation in real earnest before they could obtain the African labour which they want so much."[14] He thinks that the African should be able to choose what to accept and what to reject of Western ways, instead of being reduced to a state of serfdom by foreign and oppressive laws. He ends on a warning note, saying that the African will not accept serfdom for ever. "He realises that he must fight unceasingly for his own complete emancipation; for without this he is doomed to remain the prey of rival imperialisms, which in every successive year will drive their fangs more deeply into his vitality and strength."

Facing Mount Kenya is not a comfortable book. It contains stretches of detached urbanity, and moments of humour and light sarcasm, but it is the sudden flashes of

[13] *Ibid.*, pp. 269–70.   [14] *Ibid.*, p. 318.

white-hot anger, of bitterness, of self-pity, and sometimes of desperation which set the tone. The extracts which have been quoted here say much about Jomo Kenyatta, as well as Britain and the condition of his tribe, particularly when it is remembered that he had not been in Britain for more than six years. To a large extent this is a book about Kenyatta himself, but he also spoke as a Kikuyu for the Kikuyu, as was amply demonstrated by his popularity when he returned to Kenya.

The reader who has never been to Kenya may well ask if Kenyatta's accusations are true. On the whole they are justified by historical facts. The British in Kenya acted with all the aggressive pride that might be expected to have clung to a nation that had risen by industrial achievement to the front rank of world powers. This pride permeated both the settlers and the administrators, and even many of the missionaries. They could not believe that there could be a better economic system, a better form of government, or a better religion, than their own. The apparent initial compliance of the African to this superiority merely confirmed the attitude, and encouraged contempt for African customs and Africans in general. Faced with this inexorably demoralising position of power, the average European, often a man who would never have been noticed in his own country, lost his sense of balance. He began to believe that he really was what the African at first took him to be, a superior being with special gifts.

Once this myth took root he had acquired a vested interest in it and could only let it go at the expense of his new and comfortable way of life. The educated African was a direct challenge to this myth, and hence to the way of life, because he set out to show that the African too could be as good and as civilized as the European. An historical moment of genuine psychological superiority had led to its false perpetuation in a myth, which encouraged a pattern of economic and social superiority, which in turn, because it was based on a lie, gave rise to a defensive feeling of guilt that was afraid of being exposed. The only person who could expose it was the "mission boy." At all costs the "mission boy" must be seen to possess "only a thin veneer of civilization," and to remain at heart a savage, thus proving that real civilization needs two thousand years in which to develop. But vice, and myths are a kind of psychological vice, must make ever bigger sacrifices to the intrinsic sanity of human nature.

In the old days, when human cultures were cut off from each other, once a civilization got caught in this vicious circle of power, myth and social guilt, there was no other way out but decadence and violence, followed by yet another painful advance of the human spirit. But today, thanks to the annihilation of distance, there is no need for a small cultural group to suffer the full consequences of its own weakness. World opinion can act as a kind of international Alcoholics Anonymous and save the victim from himself. Kenya was to escape the full consequence of her madness, but not until the myth of white superiority had degenerated into a nightmare which claimed several thousand victims, including the reputation of the most influential and talented "mission boy" of them all, Jomo Kenyatta. For those who wish to move clear of the assumptions which cling like barnacles to the splendid old passenger boat called Western civilization, Kenya is not the land of "profit and sport" of Lord Cranworth; nor the green and pleasant place with smiling black faces, of books by chatty settlers' wives; but a land in which ordinary people from different cultural backgrounds had, and have, to live out one of the fiercest tests of human nature in this age.

Had there been the men to listen, the words of *Facing Mount Kenya* could have rescued Kenya from her progressive decline into racial conflict, but her rulers paid more attention to coffee prices than to the "civilizing mission," and, anyway, Europe was sliding into the second catastrophic war in twenty-five years. The vagaries of Europe's political jungle resulted in six more years of comparative calm in Kenya and colonial Africa. England's storm had gathered and gone by the time Kenya got hers. Jomo Kenyatta had six more years in which to think, inactively, about the fate of his tribe, and of himself.

CHAPTER SEVEN

THE BLUE-BOOK REBEL

ACCORDING TO his friend, Dinah Stock, Kenyatta was in quite close contact with the Kikuyu Central Association right up to the time when it was proscribed, at the beginning of the war, for allegedly subverting the Kenya Government's war effort. When the K.C.A. had to deal with some particular government policy with which they disagreed, such as the attempt to de-stock part of the Kamba tribe's reserve, they sent a cable to Kenyatta and, if appropriate, he would draw up a memorandum on the subject and give it to Arthur Creech Jones, the Labour party's spokesman on colonial affairs; or write a letter to an influential liberal paper like the *Manchester Guardian*. The war and the proscription of the K.C.A. also cut Kenyatta off from the periodic supplies of cash which were sent from Kenya. His life as a kind of respectable "Agitator Extraordinary" at the heart of the Empire came to an end, and, not for the last time in his life, he became a silent leader in exile.

Those who recognize, perhaps grudgingly, that kind and often whimsical streak which lies beneath the official calm of the British character are often puzzled by Britain's treatment of "agitators." In London, the capital of the largest empire which the world has ever seen, passionate men, outraged by the wrongs done to their countrymen in far-off colonies, could stamp their feet, thump tables, pour forth torrents of abuse, and survive to do it again the next day. They were even listened to sometimes, but with that slightly worried indulgence which is more dampening even than a London fog. Most "agitators" either returned to the more comforting hysteria of their homeland, or went mad, or succumbed and diverted their energies to football pools and the pubs. No wonder many Africans believe that some mysterious change comes over an English person as soon as he sets foot on African soil. Jomo Kenyatta came close to losing his passion in England.

In 1939 Kenyatta was living in poor lodgings in the Kings Cross area of London, close to a number of his friends. Many of these were members of the Workers' Educational Association and they found him work as a lecturer in anthropology. It was at this time that he met his future wife, Edna Grace Clarke, who was also a teacher.

When war broke out Dinah Stock, another teacher with the W.E.A., arranged for Kenyatta and some others to stay at the small Sussex village of Storrington, about forty miles south of London. She herself visited them during her holidays from a teachers' training college in Yorkshire. She told me that Kenyatta started by getting a job on a farm: "first on a general, non-mechanized farm where he could learn the ropes thoroughly, and then in a tomato house. He was a terrific worker, popular company at the pub of an evening, and managed at the same time to take a W.E.A. class and one or two Army Education courses, on African affairs, and keep chickens and grow vegetables.

"We discussed Africa a lot," she continued, "and one of his lines of thought was a plan for a pamphlet for his people, *Spear and Diplomacy*. The gist of this was: 'You are a warrior; a good warrior prides himself on mastering the most efficient weapons of the day. In our day the most efficient weapon is not the spear, nor yet the gun or the bomb; it is diplomacy. The British conquered Kenya with blue books and parliamentary reports; disheartening weapons, but master them; beat them at their own game; organize; gather your statistics, prepare your memoranda till they haven't a leg left to stand on in the eyes of the world.'" This assessment was accurate as far as most of the British colonial empire was concerned but the blue books were to break through the prejudices which besieged Kenya just too late to save some of the inhabitants.

Dinah Stock mentioned one recollection which, though trivial in itself, adds a little to a picture of that side of Kenyatta which demanded a rich measure of enjoyment from life. "He enjoyed good living," she said, "as much as anyone I've ever met; and was not incapable in wartime of wolfing the week's sugar ration, and was a superb cook. But when food was scarce I have seen him contentedly making a meal of sour milk and breadcrumbs."

Jomo Kenyatta's imposing dark figure won him even more notice in the village of Storrington than it had done in London or Birmingham. Very few of the villagers had ever seen a black man before, and they seem to have taken some local pride in harbouring someone so exotic in their midst. He had a number of friends, both among the small intellectual circle connected with the W.E.A., and with the ordinary people in the village. A bricklayer remembers how he used to come and discuss gardening with him and borrow tools and plants for his garden. Kenyatta spent a lot of time and energy making a garden out of a swampy patch in the grounds of the house where he stayed. His fellow-workmen among the tomatoes and greenhouses and the mushroom beds remember him as a quiet and pleasant person. He seldom spoke of Kenya to them.

Thoughts of Kenya's pass laws, land, and the colour bar must have been far from his mind as he used to spend those war evenings sitting by the stove in a local pub called the White Horse, drinking brown ale with the well-known composer, Arnold Bax, who was a neighbour throughout the war. There is no evidence to suggest that he was drinking to excess at this time. He was nicknamed "Jumbo" by some of the villagers, and this mysterious stranger from the other end of the world left behind him when he went a feeling of friendliness. A garage proprietor commented simply, "He never made no bother 'ere like he seem to have done over there." Hardly anyone who knew him found it easy to believe that he could have led Mau Mau, but a prominent member of the local Labour party, Arthur Johnson, had his doubts. He thought that for such an intelligent man Jomo Kenyatta had a pronounced irrational streak. He used, according to Arthur Johnson, to be aggressive about his African race, praising the warlike prowess of his Masai ancestors, and boasting about his aristocratic background. He was apparently overjoyed when his son developed a gap between his front teeth, a sign of good birth among the Masai. In England, a country where national and military pride were assuming inflated proportions, this may seem meagre evidence of irrationality.

There are two women still living near Storrington whose memories of Jomo Kenyatta are tinged with awe. One evening during the war they entered the White Horse and, over their drinks, they discussed a recalcitrant German lodger who was making their lives a misery — and who had in fact driven them to the sanctuary of the pub. If only they could get rid of him, they complained, how easy life would be. A good-looking African who was sitting quietly in the corner of the room, could not help overhearing their conversation, and smiling at one of them, he apologized for doing so. "Well, there is nothing private about it," she replied; "it's a wretched business, and neither pleading nor threats will make him go." The African expressed his sympathy, and after a moment's silence he said quietly, "Give me his name and address, and I will see to the matter." Laughing unbelievably they gave it to him, asking him when it would happen. "On Wednesday," he replied, "by telegram." And with that he rose to his feet, bowed, and went out into the street swinging his cane.

Wondering half-skeptically what kind of strange magic they were up against, the two friends thought no more about it. But towards evening on the following Wednesday they saw a telegraph boy coming up the garden path. Sure enough the telegram was for the lodger. He read it twice, then, ashen-faced, he told them he had to leave, dashed up to his room, and within half an hour he had gone — for ever. The African, who was Jomo Kenyatta, never told them what was in the telegram.

In 1943 he married Edna Grace Clarke, who was then working as a governess near Storrington. It was a strange match in some ways. She was quietly handsome and apparently conventional, while he was lively and self-assertive. Kenyatta told her frankly that if and when he had to choose between her and Kenya he would have to go. She was very devoted to him, however, and since his departure for Kenya in 1946 both she and their son, Peter, have remained completely loyal.

Although before this marriage Kenyatta had enjoyed going to local dances, he now became quieter and led the regular life of a domesticated husband. He would bicycle to work at the nursery-gardens, and in the evenings on his way home he used to pick up his son, Peter, from nursery school.

He carried on with much of his W.E.A. work, lecturing to an odd assortment of groups in the neighbourhood; army classes at Petworth, adult education groups in the villages, and even religious gatherings. His subject was always the same — Kenya — but he had the knack of varying his style and approach to suit his listeners. His methods of dealing with critical interruptions and arguments were urbane and often witty. An indignant outburst at the barbarism and superstition of the Kikuyu would be met by a scornful reference to black cats, ladders, and other objects of British superstition. He seemed to be aware of the strongly nationalist spirit engendered by the war, and he never delivered impassioned tirades against the evils of white civilization, although he was often persuasively critical of colonial administration.

Kenyatta's friend from the local Labour party, Arthur Johnson, says that the majority of his audience were normally farmers and farm workers and he admired the way in which Kenyatta won their interest and sympathy for the agricultural problems of Kikuyu — their land hunger and the limited opportunities they had for improving their stock. He quickly found that restraint and humour won him more support than bitter orations. He succeeded in making the whole process of colonial exploitation look ridiculous when he told them: "You see, the British dig for gold in a hole in Kenya, then bring it back here and lock it up in another hole. If it was left for the Kikuyu the women would make for themselves beautiful earrings."

But not all his audience shared the same appreciation of Kenyatta's down-to-earth descriptions of tribal life. A

friend of his remembers with great glee the shocked indignation with which members of the Littlehampton Co-
operative Ladies Guild listened to a detailed description of
the initiation rites of Kikuyu girls. The subject of female
circumcision, often selected by Englishmen as proof of the
barbarous habits of the Kikuyu, always aroused in Kenyatta an ardent defence of the custom. He retained a fierce
criticism of the way the missionaries in Kenya had tried to
suppress female circumcision without first understanding
the important part it played in the life of the tribe. It
appears that Kenyatta grew increasingly bitter about the
role of the missionaries, although he always conceded that
they were misguided rather than malicious.

His employer in Storrington, a self-made and extremely
vigorous man, made a gesture one day and invited Kenyatta to dinner at his home. It was not a success. He complained that Jomo Kenyatta was aggressive, argumentative,
and altogether a very difficult guest. For his part, Kenyatta
mentioned afterwards to a friend that he thought his employer had the English equivalent of a Russian "kulak"
mentality.

Another near neighbor of Jomo Kenyatta saw a rather
different side of him. "It is odd to reflect," she writes,[1] "that,
of all people on earth, Jomo Kenyatta was especially sympathetic. He had a brave and devoted white wife and a
small son who was most appealing and whom he adored.
Handsome, magnetic, debonair, Jomo had bright eyes
which glittered like diamonds above the sensual mouth and
the pointed beard, set wide apart in his dark skin. I think,
now, they were the eyes of a fanatic but when I knew him
during those war years they were usually alight with laughter rather than afire with zeal, for he had a fine sense of

[1] Extracts from the unfinished autobiography of Vera Denis-Earle.

fun . . . He preached austerity and practised self-indul-
gence, demanding the best of both worlds . . . He argued
well, loved power, had great personal ambition and a certain flashy but not really offensive flamboyance . . . Moreover, at that period anyway, physical cruelty appalled this
man . . ." She mentions too that once when she quoted to
Kenyatta, "Give me the young, and I will give you a new
heaven and a new earth," he was greatly impressed and
made a note of the words.

Not surprisingly, Kenyatta felt utterly detached from
the war and its aims, and considered that his time was
largely wasted. In Storrington he was reasonably popular,
had an outlet for his histrionic ability, and led quite a comfortable life within the existing wartime conditions. But
the roots of his being were still unattended. While Western
Europe writhed in conflict all around him, his personal
background and that of his tribe remained as a kind of
unacknowledged orphan under the tutelage of an aloof
and unimaginative aunt. The aunt had proved not to be
quite the paragon of virtue at first supposed, and the orphan was growing conscious of his own powers. Convinc-
ing kindly Sussex farm workers of the sufferings of the
Kikuyu tribe was a poor tranquillizer for a man of his
capacity and feeling. Thousands of miles away in Kenya
colonial life pursued its seemingly unalterable course, and
other and younger "mission boys" were emerging every
year into a society which offered them the full status of
manhood, in a hundred years or so, when they were "fully
civilized." The technical and allegedly spiritual poverty of
Africa continued to serve as a somewhat bewildering pre-
text for Europe to postpone once again a long overdue
examination of her own nature and purpose. A platform
ticket seemed an ungracious reward from the "civilizing

mission" after displaying all those travel posters so allur-
ingly before the eyes of young Africa.

When the war ended, Jomo Kenyatta quickly resumed
contact with his political associates and he spent less and
less time at home. He soon became closely concerned with
the Pan-Africa Movement, which was centred on Manchester and attracted a growing number of politically conscious Africans and Negroes. Among these were Kwame
Nkrumah, George Padmore, T. R. Mackonnen, and Peter
Abrahams. Taking advantage of the presence of many
socialist leaders in Britain for the World Trades Union
Conference, George Padmore, then the chairman of the
International African Service Bureau, suggested the organization of a Pan-African Congress. The idea was taken
up by Dr. Peter Milliard, a Negro physician in practise in
Manchester. Throughout the summer of 1945 Jomo Kenyatta spent as much time as possible in Manchester, helping Padmore and Nkrumah, who were joint secretaries of
the Organizing Committee.

On October 13 of that year the Congress was opened by
the Lord Mayor of Manchester in the Town Hall, and continued for eight days. Over two hundred delegates from
all over the world attended, under the joint chairmanship
of Dr. W. E. Dubois, an American Negro scholar and a
founder-member of the National Association for the Advancement of Coloured Peoples, and Dr. Milliard, the
chairman of the recently formed British section of the Pan-
African Federation. Kenyatta attended as General Secretary of the Kikuyu Central Association (still banned in
Kenya), and was made chairman of the Credentials Committee and *rapporteur* of the East African section.

Kenyatta did not express militant anti-European views at

the Congress. He said he recognized the value of European energy in Kenya and hoped that, after independence, Europeans would stay and become integrated under some form of socialism. Other views expressed at this Congress, the fifth of its kind, reflected support for the liberal democratic principles set out in the Declaration of Human Rights and the Atlantic Charter. A resolution was passed unanimously sponsoring the doctrine of African socialism based on the tactics of "positive non-violent action." Unlike its predecessors, which had taken place between 1919 and 1927, and included a high proportion of intellectual reformists from the middle class, this Congress reflected the awakening consciousness of the dependent countries, and many delegates were students and unskilled workers.

After the Congress Kenyatta stayed on in Manchester with Makonnen and Milliard to organize the Pan-African Federation. Nkrumah was made secretary of the Working Committee, and the main purpose of the federation became that of co-ordinating the various political movements for independence which were springing up in the colonies. An attempt to find a London headquarters for the movement failed.

Kenyatta's usefulness in England as a spokesman for his people had obviously now come to an end. Whitehall would be more likely to change its mind on colonial policy if it was faced in the colonies with massive popular organizations which could not be contained even by force. As a political one-man band Kenyatta had had a limited success in converting intellectual liberals to his cause, but he had never succeeded in really influencing British Government policy. The return of the Labour party to power in England at the end of the war raised the hopes of many

African politicians that at last there would be a significant change in policy, and in 1945 Kenyatta applied for permission to return to Kenya.

These hopes were quickly dashed when it became evident that immediate independence was not to be granted. In February of 1946 both Kenyatta and Nkrumah expressed their bitter disappointment in a strong attack on the Labour spokesman on colonial affairs, Arthur Creech Jones, at a week-end school organized by the Fabian Commonwealth Bureau. All African exiles did not share this disappointment, however, and one particular friend of Kenyatta's, the writer Peter Abrahams, broke with him over this issue. In September 1946, with little or no warning to his friends, or even his family, Jomo Kenyatta sailed for Mombasa.

More than sixteen years in Europe had left their mark on the brash, excitable young man who had come to England in 1929. He was now a mature man well into middle age. His alert and graceful figure had become heavy and solid. The warrior fingering the tip of a spear reflectively, almost longingly, of an early studio photo had become the apostle of blue-book revolution based on socialist nonviolent principles. The exuberant dandy had developed into a man of sensual maturity. He was too African to allow his life to be enslaved by intellectual gods in the way of many European social and political rebels. No longer was he the victim of ignorance of English and English customs. In fact he had proved so adaptable that it must have been a real temptation to stay on in England and fight the revolution from the nonviolent refuge of an armchair in Storrington. But although the superstructure of Kenyatta's life had developed into a formidable whole, it was still based on an uneasy mixture of uncertainty and anger. Neither his own origin, nor that of his tribe, nor that of Africa, had yet won full acceptance on the world's stage. Until this happened Kenyatta's peace, and that of his tribe, and of Africa, would be a deluding sham.

Europe, another principal actor in the Kenya pantomime, had been terribly mauled by the events of these years. From one war, which quickly exchanged chivalry for wholesale slaughter in subhuman conditions, the Continent had drifted through economic anarchy and "ideological debauchery" (a phrase of Arthur Koestler, himself deeply involved at that time) into political hysteria and yet another world war. Violence had become the price of a prolonged escape from the laws of human nature into a realm where utility ruled over humility and humanity.

This time the gods had raised the price. The death of thousands of young men was no longer enough. The grey shroud covered men, women, and children, with impartiality, and by the million. It needed the catastrophic blast of an atomic bomb to penetrate the blunted senses of mankind. Punch-drunk, a plea of justifiable homicide was entered by the participants, and it seemed that the same disastrous course was to be followed once more. Atomic bombs became hydrogen bombs. Western civilized man, who had shown unprecedented talent for unravelling the mysteries of science, was once again peering blindly over the edge of the abyss which his lust for power had created. Once again the only balance he could conceive of to help him was the "balance of terror." His god was the "new Baal, lording it over the moral vacuum with his electronic brain."[2]

[2] *The Sleepwalkers*, Arthur Koestler, p. 542.

But within this macabre framework there were positive forces at work, which found expression in the Declaration of Human Rights and the founding of the United Nations. The peoples of the colonial territories, as yet untried on the world stage, recognized in these constructive moves their means of escape into adulthood. But the colonies, as always, were behind the times, and the Western civilization which welcomed Kenyatta in Mombasa have few traces of the new ideas.

CHAPTER EIGHT

DISHEARTENING WEAPONS

WHEN JOMO KENYATTA landed at Mombasa in September 1946, he is said to have knelt and kissed the soil of Kenya. Such an act, if true, although deprived of some of its romance by the unappealing concrete of Mombasa docks, would have been typical of his sense of the dramatic. Although his sixteen years in England had seldom been dull and had given him some valuable experience, there must have been many moments when his expressive nature found it hard to fit in with the strict reservations of the English character. To see the blue skies of East Africa again, and the rich green background of Mombasa, and to breathe the heavy warm air, must have been a moment of strong emotion for him. And he was bringing back with him to the Kikuyu people not only his own varied experience of Western culture but the heady news of postwar political developments. The Atlantic Charter and the Declaration of Human Rights were powerful ammunition for a nationalist in an English colony, and Kenyatta knew that he had the technique to use it.

But the Kenya he found in 1946 was an unhappy place, despite its superficial air of gaiety, and racial tension was increasing. He soon found that blue-book diplomacy was of little use in this emotional atmosphere. Seven short years later a British magistrate was to say to Jomo Kenyatta, after one of the most publicized trials in Africa: "I do not believe you. It is my belief that soon after your long stay in Europe and when you came back to this Colony you commenced to organize this Mau Mau society, the object of which was to drive out from Kenya all Europeans, and in doing so to kill them if necessary. I am satisfied that the master mind behind this plan was yours." Soon afterwards, on September 8, 1954, a news item in the London *Times* announced briefly: "Jomo Kenyatta will probably spend the rest of his life in the remote Northern Frontier District of Kenya." The intervening years, looking back on them now, have something of the relentless progression of a Greek tragedy.

The Kenya which Jomo Kenyatta found on his return had changed in many respects from the small-time colony he had left behind in 1931. Kenya politics had evolved from the comic-opera irresponsibility of the early years into a less rowdy but still serious tug-of-war between the settlers and the British officials. Slowly but surely, with occasional minor setbacks, the settlers had been gaining ground. Despite the rejection by the British Government of the idea of a federation of East Africa — a move comparable to the federation of Central Africa in later years — and despite occasional statements that the British Government would maintain its self-appointed position as guardian of the African people, the settlers won more than they lost.

After their defeat of the political challenge by the numerically superior Indian population, and having won the dominating voice in the allocation of public funds, their next victory had lain in the results of the Carter Commission on land. Although they would like to have had the whole of Kenya thrown open eventually to the principles of free enterprise on their terms, they were quite happy that the Commission drew a legal line round the White Highlands and made no attempt to meet the future land requirements of the growing African population.

In 1937 the settlers agreed, after years of blunt refusal, to pay a light income tax, but they demanded heavy compensation for this piece of civil gallantry. They ensured that in return they should have a representation in the Legislative Council out of all proportion to their numbers. The Colonial Office in London still had a deciding voice, but the settlers had as many members as were nominated by the Government, and twice the number allotted to the Indians. The five million Africans were represented by two nominated Europeans, the first African not being nominated until 1945. In 1937, despite strong objections from local Africans, a further small area of land near Nairobi was taken out of the Kikuyu Reserve and added to the White Highlands. It was small in terms of square miles but far-reaching in its effect on deteriorating African confidence in white pledges and motives.

Between 1931 and 1948 the settler population had nearly doubled, and now stood at 30,000. After the war their dislike of Colonial Office rule was as fervent as ever. Writing in the local paper in 1946, a farmer said: "The time has now arrived for our Elected Members to be inspired by constructive imagination and vision that will conduct Kenya from Colonial Office tyranny to a constitutional freedom which is the legitimate aspiration of all freedom and liberty loving peoples." These words could have been used by an African nationalist in more recent years, but his meaning would have been different. The farmer wanted freedom to rule, not only himself and the other settlers, but the entire population of Africans and Indians as well. He wanted to turn the slow, but ultimately progressive, rule of the Colonial Office into a full-blown white dictatorship on the lines of South Africa. Few Africans, even at that date, envisaged self-government with an African majority, and, faced with the alternative of Colonial Office or settler rule, they unanimously chose the former. The myth of white supremacy had not yet been brutally dissipated by events, and there was still time for it to be firmly but gently deflated by a strong liberal policy from London.

African politics remained a weak force, and nationalism, as distinct from tribalism, was in its infancy when Kenyatta returned. Hampered by lack of education and experience, by the long tradition of tribalism, as well as by laws which restricted movement and assembly, and faced with a powerful settler clique, African politicians had achieved very little. Even the Kikuyu Central Association, which had done as well as could be expected over the land issue, had failed to win the active support of the whole tribe, before it was suppressed at the beginning of the war. Without the means of expressing themselves either verbally or organizationally in European terms, African politics easily degenerated into groups of rival factions. If Britain had learnt the lessons of her own past, more effort might have been made to guide the inevitable spread of African political interest into well-constructed and legitimate channels.

Economically Kenya had had a rough time over the years, like all small countries dependent on basic agricultural exports in a world market which was at the mercy of unpredictable fluctuations. But the settlers, who made up in initiative and energy something of what they lacked in political vision, had survived all the storms, and Kenya's national income showed a steady rise. One farmer, who today has a prosperous farm, used to make a living during the slump in the early thirties by selling baboons to American laboratories and cheetah to Indian maharajahs. However, very little of the increasing wealth, whether from baboons or coffee, went into the pockets of Africans, who, by devious means, had been prevented from growing coffee, the one crop which fetched a continuously good price.

Those Africans who lived within the old tribal framework at least had enough to eat, but conditions in Nairobi were bad, and getting worse. Even as late as 1955 the East African Royal Commission found that only 5 per cent of African workers in the city had an income which could support a normal family, and said, "the conditions of life for . . . the majority of the Africans in the towns have been deteriorating over a considerable period . . . Moreover their deterioration has not yet been arrested." A Kikuyu woman who worked for the Nairobi Municipal Council in 1945 as a social welfare assistant told me that her pay of 50 shillings per month, with housing added, was so little that she often had nothing but a cup of tea to keep her going from the time she got up until her work ended. With its startling gap between rich and poor, Nairobi was passing through the same stage of social and economic chaos as the towns of industrial England a hundred years before. Just as others did then, people in Nairobi shook their heads helplessly. It required Mau Mau to challenge their impotence.

Religiously too, the African in the Kenya of 1947 was in a desperate state. A former Government psychiatrist described the situation as "psychologically chaotic."[1] Because the impact of white rule had been felt most strongly by the Kikuyu, it was they who bore the brunt of this chaos. Elspeth Huxley uses one of her heroines to express her own consciousness of this spiritual breakdown:

[1] *The Psychology of Mau Mau*, Dr. J. C. Carothers, M.B., D.P.M., Government Printer, Nairobi, p. 7.

She was afraid that something like that was happening
to many of the Kikuyu she had grown up among and loved.
They were a people who felt the presence of the spirit
everywhere, in trees and rocks and forests, above all in
Kere-Nyaga's snows. Often she had felt the truth of their
belief when she had seen the peak standing out, pencilled
lightly against dawn or sunset, and when she walked in
forest shadows and along the streams. This country was
spirit-haunted as ancient Greece had been, and she shared
its people's sensitivity to the unseen, the waiting presences
who would one day wait no longer and call the living to
join the dead and the unborn. Once they left their mountain and its green shoulders for the hard cities and alien
farms, something in them withered, like life within the
soul, and some among them turned rotten, sterile and dangerous. The power to create dies in them, they could not
feel the waiting spirit any longer, and they had in them
only the power to destroy.[2]

It is only in the light of understanding such as this that
the thousands of "detribalized" Africans in Kenya's towns
become, not simply half-baked "teddy boys," but men irretrievably cut off from one source of life and searching desperately for another.

Other men in other times and places had suffered even
greater economic hardships and loss of political liberty, and
had somehow survived. But few men in any age have had
to face such an abrupt transition as the Africans of this
time, and for far too many of them the lifebelt offered by
Western civilization had been dangled just out of reach.
To be introduced to the mysteries of modern education and
then to be told that if he tried hard he might earn the dignity due to a full adult in fifty or a hundred years was the
bleak prospect which lay before the young Kenya African
in 1946.

[2] *A Thing to Love*, Elspeth Huxley.

In reaction to this obstacle in the way of African manhood two developments had taken place, in the religious and in the educational fields. Religious sects sprang up in an attempt to forge a link between tribal beliefs and the new religion. In *Facing Mount Kenya* Kenyatta mentions the "People of God." In one tribe a footballer suddenly turned to prophecy before the war, advocated polygamy, was consigned to a mental home, and later returned home to forecast the arrival of a Black Christ who would drive away the Europeans. He was arrested in 1948 and was still in custody in 1960. His sect used the sacrifice of sheep and goats, the Protestant Bible, the Roman Catholic cross, and the Muslim habit of growing beards. In one frenzied outburst three Europeans were killed, including a District Commissioner.

Another sect among the Kikuyu, which began in 1945, believed in Christ, prayed facing Mount Kenya, wore skins, practised polygamy, and propitiated ancestors. Some of them wore turbans and took off their shoes to pray. One of their leaders was hanged after a young European police officer and two askaris were killed by members of the sect. During Mau Mau itself, a young Kikuyu deaf-mute was suddenly cured. He whipped up a crowd in a village by telling them that God would arrive at 1 P.M. to destroy the Government and that bullets would turn to water. After a fight with the police, sixteen Kikuyu were dead and seventeen injured. In 1960 there was a Kikuyu sect with thousands of supporters that had its own prophets and refused to shake hands with Europeans. One thing that characterizes most of these sects is an acceptance of the truth of Christ, a hatred of European rule, and a pathetic inability to acknowledge the facts of modern life. For every one man who was committed to one of these sects there must have been hundreds who were on the side lines, undecided, and almost equally lost.

In the educational field, the Kikuyu Independent Schools had grown up as a direct result of an attempt by missionaries to change the custom of female circumcision. When Kenyatta returned in 1946 he found more than three hundred schools educating about 60,000 children. Some of the schools taught Christianity, without the help of Europeans, and retained some loyalty for the Government. Others were traditional in their religious allegiances, and did all they could to do without Government aid or interference. All were poor, and by European standards both the teaching and the facilities were of a low standard. In 1939 Peter Koinange, who had attended universities in both Britain and the United States, set up a Teachers' Training College at the Kikuyu village of Githunguri, and he had high ambitions to develop African education to university level. This college later became the target of Government investigation into Mau Mau.

But there was something sad and hopeless about all these ventures, political, educational, and religious. At the best there was an air of bravado about them; a cheerful determination to prove that Africans were human beings with the same abilities as others. At the worst they reflected a flight from the present, with all its crippling pride and prejudice. The fact that many of the most intelligent and capable Africans were involved is an indication of the extent to which the Government had lost touch with its most politically valuable citizens. In their watertight community, with its clubs, its golf, and its built-in sense of national superiority, few Europeans had any conception of the psychological chaos which lay around them. Like the passengers on the doomed *Titanic*, they did not see where they were going.

Jomo Kenyatta was too intelligent a man not to sense quickly the dangerous degree of confusion into which Kenya had drifted. It was one thing to recognize it, though, and a good deal more difficult to do anything about it. "We are unwilling to starve any longer," the African leaders had announced defiantly, at the postwar Pan-African Congress in Birmingham, "while doing the world's drudgery, in order to support, by our poverty and ignorance, a false aristocracy and a discredited imperialism. All colonies must be free from foreign imperialist control, whether political or economic." Fine words, but what was to be done about them in Kenya? The aristocrats were false and the imperialists were largely discredited, but neither realized it. The latter dimly sensed the wide implications of the United Nations and the Declaration of Human Rights, but the former had embalmed its myth in hard cash and political privilege, and was not to be budged by words. In the postwar world most leading Africans quickly ceased to believe in white leadership, and after a brief flirtation with the idea of sharing power, the irresistible necessity for political independence became clearer and more urgent.

In Ghana (then the Gold Coast) Kenyatta's friend, Nkrumah, had his own problems. In Kenya Jomo Kenyatta had somehow to build up the pathetically insufficient African political, educational, and religious organizations into a force which could override the hesitations of the Colonial Office and the powerful irrationality of settlerdom. It was a Herculean task, and Kenyatta must have felt at times like a sprinter trying to run the hundred yards in treacle.

Soon after he had arrived in Nairobi, Kenyatta visited

the Governor, Sir Philip Mitchell. It was a fateful meeting.
Kenyatta told Sir Philip that he wanted to take an active
part in politics, and the response was that he should first
acclimatize himself to the current situation in Kenya by
entering into local government, and then later move into
the wider sphere of national politics. On the face of it this
suggestion was quite sensible, but it left out of account the
dominating factor in all nationalist politics — emotion.
Jomo Kenyatta was a man well into middle age by this
time, and someone who had earned a place in his own
right amongst the intelligentsia in England. He was acutely
aware not only of the strength but of the weakness in
Western civilization and saw straight through the element
of sham in colonial pretensions. He had already had some
experience of his capacity as a leader, and was fired with
the postwar surge of optimism and ambition among coloured people. But time was not on his side. He needed
instant recognition both for himself and his people. To be
offered a place on a local African District Council, under
the chairmanship of an English District Commissioner
whose main preoccupations were roads, accounts, and
minor law cases, was like proposing to sail the *Queen Mary*
in a duck-pond. Kenyatta turned down the suggestion.

If the Governor had made an immediate offer to nomi-
nate Kenyatta to the Legislative Council, it is just possible
that he would have been able to control those former
members of the K.C.A. who were opposed to any co-operation with the Government. But it is extremely doubtful if
this would have had any real effect on the future course
of events. Kenyatta would have soon found, as did men
like Eliud Mathu, the first Kikuyu nominated member, that
eloquence had little effect, and he would have resigned. In
any case, with rare exceptions, British Colonial Governors,

like their officials, shared the current middle-class English distaste for politics, and it would have been out of character for Sir Philip Mitchell to sense the urgency behind the new nationalism. Even the Labour Government in Britain, with all its brave past of anti-colonialist ideals, failed to come to grips with the problem.

From this time on, Jomo Kenyatta became a hostage to his environment. He could shape and colour events to some extent, but he had little or no control over their direction. The European myth had set like concrete in Kenya, and the inevitable clash of undirected emotions could only be averted by a Christ or a Gandhi, or by the Labour Government in London. There was no Christ and no Gandhi, and the Labour party was itself a prey to the lack of self-confidence of postwar Europe.

Jomo Kenyatta quickly set to work to build up that massive demonstration of African unity which he and Nkrumah had decided in London was the only way of winning political independence and the right to be African. He found an embryo national organization in the Kenya African Union, which had evolved from the Kenya African Study Union. The latter had been started in 1944 by the newly nominated African member of Legislative Council, Eliud Mathu, and its aims were to unite the African people and to foster their social, economic, and political interests. In 1946, a few months before Kenyatta's return, the Kenya African Union was formed, and the speeches at this meeting show the strength, even at this stage, of political feeling among leading Africans.

"We must have more land," said the new president, James Gichuru (still a leading figure in Kenya politics), "and this land can only be got from the so-called White Highlands." He described the Kikuyu "squatters" on Euro-

pean farms as living in a state of "modern serfdom." On the
relations between Africans and Europeans he declared that
they were generally friendly, "when the white man wants
something from us." He added that Africans had reached
the conclusion that the European had assumed a superiority
not borne out by realities, apart from his economic and
technical advantages, and said that every step the settlers
were taking was being watched. In response to a memorandum sent to the Colonial Office a few months previously, which had asked, among other things, for increased
African representation in the Legislative Council, there
had come back a suffocating bale of official wool. His Majesty's Government was fully conscious of the just aspira-
tions of the African people and was of the opinion that
legitimate demands could best be met at the present time
by profiting from experience in local government. And,
much as His Majesty's Government would like to maintain
as rapid a pace as possible in constitutional development,
it was at the same time deeply aware of its duty towards
those who were held in its trust: "It will therefore be appreciated," went on the reply, "that the protection of the
interests and rights of the African people is not a matter
which, at this stage, can be secured only, or even primarily,
by direct African representation in the Legislature, or on
public boards or committees." Once again the appropriate
moral attitude had been struck. For the annual debate in
the House of Commons on colonial affairs in 1947 there
were six hours of speeches and an average attendance of
46 out of 640 members.

On June 1, 1947, Jomo Kenyatta was elected president
of K.A.U. Although his powers of leadership were quickly
recognized by local politicians, they enforced a certain
price for their support. Some of the former members of the

banned K.C.A., men of his own age but without his wide experience, demanded that he should repay their loyal support over the years by carrying on their bitter refusal to co-operate with anything the Government did, good or bad. At first these men had been inspired by honest anger at Government refusal to meet their objections on the land issue. Anger had turned to bitterness as the years went by and some were deported for "subversion," which gave them time to brood over and magnify their grievances. Often, bitterness had become plain racial hatred, directed impartially at anything white. As one of them told me, hopelessly, "To fight for the public is to die like a dog." To oppose these men, even had he wished to, might well have been the physical as well as the political end of Kenyatta.

Another set which played an increasingly important part in these years was known as the "Forty Group," and consisted of those Kikuyu men who had come of age in 1940. Many of them had seen action during the war in far-off lands, and life in the country was now too tedious for them. Hundreds had failed to find work in Nairobi and they banded together into a rowdy group, with a potentially dangerous knowledge of modern weapons. Politics for them became a source of excitement and they quickly tagged on to the Kenyatta band wagon, providing the semi-criminal element from which no nationalist movement is free.

Apart from these two difficult groups, Kenyatta soon had in his ill-assorted following a large peasant element, and a small body of educated men who wanted "freedom," but wanted it in such a way that they could show the Europeans that Africans were responsible people. The peasants responded simply to leadership from a man whom they recognized to be intellectually powerful and personally magnetic. During his first days in Kenya people flocked to see and hear him. A reception was held at his home just outside Nairobi, and his daughter Margaret told me that among the crowds who came were many from the farthest corner of the Kikuyu Reserve.

Within two months of his arrival, the Police Special Branch reported that he had privately told people that he disliked Europeans and Asians and that in time Africa would be free of them.[3] If this is true then it shows that he had quickly settled into the conventional mould of a nationalist leader, responding at every moment to popular feeling, and encouraging it, in an effort to build up the political pressure needed to break the Government to his will. His aim was not to fight for abstract ideals, but to fight for African self-government and self-confidence. The more unrelenting the opposition, the more crude and desperate became the fight. The Kenya Government would not respond to the principles of the Atlantic Charter, but being British they could not condemn them. Thus one important weapon in Kenyatta's armoury became the language of democracy, which aroused Africans to fever pitch while the Government shook its head helplessly.

The District Commissioner of one Kikuyu district soon reported a sharp deterioration in the "morale and discipline" of his area. "The main cause of this," he said, "appears to be the return of Jomo Kenyatta to the Colony, which has been hailed by the African Press, and his starting up again, in a most virulent form, the activities of the K.C.A. It is clear that a heavy tide of subversive propaganda, which includes strong anti-European feeling and encouragement to flout the authority of Government and

[3] Corfield Report, p. 50.

local authorities, is flowing from Nairobi to the Kikuyu districts."

Eliud Mathu was claimed by the Government, rather desperately, as moderate by comparison with Kenyatta, but Mathu's well-delivered speeches in the Legislative Council were not the same as those made before an excited African audience. In 1947 he made a speech at Kakamega which should have opened the eyes of those who clung to the belief that the real African leaders were those who agreed with the Government on every important point. "We are the true inhabitants of Kenya," he said, "and the land is ours completely. We were found here by the explorers. When God made man, he gave the people of each colour their own place to live and we Africans were put here in Africa. It has been ours right from the word 'go.'" Roars and cheers greeted everything he said. "We are men," they chanted in unison three times when he told them they should remember they were human beings just like anyone else.[4]

People brought up amid the usually polite noises of political meetings in England can have little idea of the colour, excitement and clamour of a nationalist meeting in Africa. Choirs, screeching women, crying babies, and the police are all inevitable ingredients, forming a heady atmosphere which is political, religious, and social.

Mathu was later spurned because he was thought too moderate by the Africans. By the end of 1947, African nationalism was set on a course which must lead inexorably either to the end of white rule or to an explosion. An explosion followed soon afterwards, to be immediately succeeded by the ebb of white rule.

[4] *East African Standard,* July 18, 1947.

Apart from politics, Kenyatta quickly gained control of the Kikuyu Independent Schools, and moved to Githunguri where the Teachers' Training College was situated. He sometimes did some teaching himself and his pupils were as impressed by his obvious talent as had been the students of anthropology in London and the Sussex farm workers of Storrington.

At about this time he was visited by an American journalist, Negley Farson, who was a strong though sometimes critical admirer of the British. He describes Kenyatta as "a big paunchy man, bearded, with slightly bloodshot eyes, a theatrically monstrous ebony elephant-headed walking stick, a gold-rimmed cornelian signet ring about the size of a napkin ring, an outsize gold wrist watch fastened to his hefty arm with a gold strap, dressed in European tweed jacket and flannel slacks — with as pleasant, wary and ingratiating a manner as you have ever met . . . a born actor, an evident leader, and perhaps just because of this, a man born for trouble."[5]

The Government had launched a scheme to conserve soil by terracing in the Kikuyu reserve, and Kenyatta had been accused of sabotaging the plan by persuading the Kikuyu women not to take part. Negley Farson asked him:

"Tell me, Mr. Kenyatta, why did you stop the terracing at Fort Hall?"

"I *never* tried to stop the terracing at Fort Hall!"

Jomo sat up. There had been something disarming in his injured surprise, almost a lamentation; and now, actor that he is, those eyes of his travelled from my wife's face to mine. And what eyes! They made me think of Leo Slezak, the great Hungarian tenor, when he was playing Othello, and I had watched him bending over Desdemona, through

[5] *Last Chance in Africa*, Negley Farson, p. 113.

my peep-hole in the back-drop. Jomo's eyes came to rest on the astounded ground between us: "Why I'd never do anything so silly as that!"

"Well, who did then? Because somebody told them to stop."

"Unh-hunh? Well, it's just like I was telling you . . . these young men — they call themselves the 'Forty's' — they came out from Nairobi, and *they* told the people of Fort Hall that I had given the order to stop terracing. I never said anything."[6]

Negley Farson never came to a definite conclusion as to whether Kenyatta had or had not stopped this scheme. But it is certain that he would not have allowed an agricultural scheme, however beneficial economically, to stand between him and his goal of independence. To a nationalist smarting under foreign superiority, even the most obviously useful foreign innovations easily appear as a maddening excuse for continued superiority. The swing from love to hate is a short quick movement in a colony, and Europeans in Kenya were beginning to reap the harvest they had sown. The extent to which suspicion had begun to obscure every issue is illustrated by the example of the Karatina Canning Factory, set up in the war to supply the Army with tinned vegetables. After the war the Government proposed to hand it over to a British firm, which would operate it with the help of a board of Europeans and Africans. But the local Kikuyu farmers said they wanted to run it themselves, and after much discussion the Chief Native Commissioner decided to abandon the scheme altogether. This has been quoted as an example of African political irresponsibility, but there is another side to it. A retired civil servant, well known for his fearless criticism of

6 *Ibid.*, p. 114.

the Government, told me that he had tried to persuade the
Chief Native Commissioner to allow the Kikuyu to try to
run the factory themselves, and learn by hard experience
— but paternalism had won.

At his house in Githunguri, Kenyatta led a comfortable
life. His seven-room thatch-roofed house was surrounded
by a bamboo stockade, and on the lawn was a symbolic
arrangement of two spears and a shield. The library contained books by H. G. Wells, Galsworthy, Chesterton,
Nietzsche, and Schopenhauer, and there was a picture of
his old friend Paul Robeson. Kenyatta still continued to
practice his skill as a cook.

As for the college itself, it was housed in simple huts,
and the staff seem to have made up in enthusiasm what
they lacked in academic attainment. Negley Farson describes a gymnastic display there as the "most inspiring
exhibition that I saw anywhere in Kenya." There were
many tribes represented among the pupils and he wrote
that the "brotherly feeling" among them was "exhilarat-
ing." "The first book I picked up," he wrote, "on entering
one of these wattle-and-mud classrooms was *Race Conflicts in Africa*. And I am sure that when, or if, his young
pupils ever graduate — and they come from all parts of
Kenya, from nearly all the tribes — they will teach the
young Africans more of what is in such a book than what
the Iron Duke did to Napoleon at Waterloo."

He looked beneath the superficial prosperity of Nairobi
at the "black hooliganism" which was rife, and said that
the steel mesh which guarded the windows and doors of
European houses "makes you feel like white exhibits in a
black man's zoo." He commented on the effect which
Africa seemed to have on otherwise ordinary Europeans,
and the "unbearable rudeness with which you will see the

average white man (and the women are far worse) treating the average African today." He came to the conclusion that "an education in understanding is the only thing that should be gone in for in Africa today."

Negley Farson discussed the colour bar with Kenyatta. "Until that is abolished," Kenyatta insisted, "we will *never* have any comfort between the races! Take me. Here, on this hill, I am free. I hate to go into Nairobi. I want to run away from towns. I am always afraid that some day some ignorant white man will come up to me and say: 'Here you, get out!' That might happen to me any day. . . ."[7]

On education, Kenyatta told him: "You ask me what kind of a line I am taking? Well, I think the best way to put it would be to say that I am cutting the dead wood out of a lot of our old African beliefs, and I am reinforcing what I think are some of the best things of our African way of life. I am sending them out with something that I hope is going to work. I want them to be proud of being Africans! I don't want to make a lot of Black Englishmen!"[8]

Kenyatta did not devote all his speeches to problems of land, the colour bar, and the franchise. He frequently warned his listeners that unless they learnt how to "work intelligently" they would not get the things they wanted. Negley Farson admitted, "He speaks more plain words to his own people than a white man can — for they listen."

However, Government officials still suspected him of deliberately opposing agricultural improvement schemes, although the District Commissioner of Fort Hall reported in 1947: "By October . . . Jomo Kenyatta appeared to be regretting the riotous growth which had sprung from his seeds and during the tour of the Fort Hall district with the District Commissioner he did his best to eradicate it.

[7] *Ibid.*, p. 209.   [8] *Ibid.*, p. 127.

His followers were however by then finding the new life far too pleasing to give up willingly, and Jomo Kenyatta's influence appeared to be as small as his reception was poor."

Events were beginning to slide towards a complete breakdown in government. At the end of 1947 the same D.C. sent a secret report to the Director of Intelligence in Nairobi, saying, "There is a very strong rumour circulating that all the wrongs of the Kikuyu will be simultaneously righted by the murder of all Europeans." Chiefs, who were paid officials, became the target of abuse and threats of violence. Ugly examples of intimidation occurred among the few who for one reason or another refused to contribute to fund collections for either K.A.U. or the Independent Schools. Government officials in the Kikuyu Reserve demanded firmer Government action, without much success. The Governor, the Kenya Government, and the British Government, were liberal at heart but their will to act had almost gone.

S. V. Cooke, a former District Commissioner who had often jeopardized his chances of promotion in order to say what he thought of Government policy, was now in the Legislative Council, and at the beginning of 1948 he tabled a motion, which read: "That this Council, believing that often agitation is a symptom and not a cause of unrest, views with grave concern the political situation in many of the native areas today." The motion was heavily defeated. At the end of the previous year Mr. Cooke had said, ". . . I emphatically do accuse the Administration from the top to the bottom for being largely responsible for the present chaotic state of affairs."

At the end of 1948 there were reports that former K.C.A. members were winning the support of the "squatters" on the European farms by promising them that Kenyatta would give land to all those who had taken the oath of allegiance.[9] The oaths were being administered at night, contrary to Kikuyu custom. During the next year a missionary wrote a report accusing Kenyatta of waging ideological warfare against Christianity and posing as a "saviour" who would lead his people back to the old religion.[10] In the same year Colonel Meinertzhagen, who in the first years of British settlement in Kenya had warned against the Kikuyu being allowed to brood over their grievances, sent a letter to the Governor in which he said that a Kikuyu chief had warned him that the people were very angry about European interference with their land and their customs: "He fears an outbreak of violence against Europeans, involving murders on a large scale under the direction of a secret society now in existence called 'Maw Maw,' whose influence in the tribe is rapidly growing and whose oaths, taken in utmost secrecy, are binding on those who are compelled to take them."

By 1950, when Mau Mau was officially banned, the psychological chaos among the Kikuyu tribe was degenerating into a kind of collective insanity in which reason played little or no part. "Detribalized" politicians and thugs roamed the Reserves rousing the bewildered peasants from their apathy, and enforcing oaths of secrecy which were a pathetic and lunatic distortion of the traditional tribal oaths. But it was only the aggravation of a disease which had set in much earlier. Three years before, Eliud Mathu, the "moderate," had told members of the Legislative Council:

"Those who still cherish their former freedom and common rights bitterly resent having to apply for permission to

[9] Corfield Report, p. 77.   [10] *Ibid.*, p. 80.

meet together for any purpose whatever. Naturally the law is evaded and they meet at night behind locked doors with a sentry outside; they meet in caves, in the depths of banana groves or in swampy valleys away from the habitations of their fellow men to avoid detection. Yes, they meet together, these 'free, happy Africans' of His Majesty's Colony of Kenya, like felons, with all the humiliating circumstances and methods they are forced to adopt; whispering and cursing the Europeans and their own headmen who administer an oppressive and unjustified law. One day their repressions are bound to burst out, with the usual unhappy consequences for all."

In his house at Githunguri, Jomo Kenyatta continued to teach, when he was not away at political meetings, but there were signs that he knew that his attempt to base a national political organization on the various elements in the disintegrating Kikuyu tribe was already doomed. That part of him which had won success in the disciplined intellectual world of London could play no part here. Only the actor and the Kikuyu mystic had a place. He could stimulate and he could magnetize, but he could not control or guide a people whose last links with social sanity and reason were being remorselessly eroded by rulers with a mistaken sense of duty. By 1950 the "civilizing mission" had become a tyranny of good intentions, falsely based on a racial myth.

The pressures on the personality of Kenyatta himself, caught as he was at the centre of the emotional maelstrom, were becoming more intense every month. Drink began to act as a tranquilliser for this leader with no way forward.

CHAPTER NINE

SUBSERVIENCE OR SEDITION

IT HAS been said by those who hold Kenyatta responsible for Mau Mau that, even if he did not actually plan it in all its brutal details, he had the influence to stop it before it got out of hand. But as has been seen, this would have involved not only influence but a contradiction of a part of his own nature. The political demands which he had put forward to the Kenya Government through the legitimate means of the Kenya African Union were in line with the ideals for which the West claimed to have fought the Nazis. Many Kenya Africans had also fought in this war. Kenyatta wanted his people, and himself, to have the same political freedom as that enjoyed by the English. But in Kenya he was soon made to understand that political freedom and equality with white people in a colony depended, not on human rights, but on some undefined standard of civilization, to be reached only in perhaps fifty, perhaps a hundred years' time.

This policy of gradualism built up a reaction first of disappointment, then anger, then hatred. For those with the least reserves to fall back on, mostly young men whose lives had been thrust towards the new ways by education, by the war, by their youth, retreat meant individual disaster of the first magnitude. They could not retreat into a tribal pattern of security which they had never really belonged to. Their natural instinct was to fight their way out. Anything European became the target, and the only weapons they had, apart from a few guns, were secret oaths to promote unity, and a short, wide chopping knife, which the Europeans had introduced for farm work, called a panga.

These were the men who made up the most bloodthirsty part of Kenyatta's following, and who in 1950, were beginning to enforce oaths on the more frightened peasants in the rural areas. What could Kenyatta do with them? As a leader who had identified himself with his tribe, and with the cause of African dignity, he had a strong sympathy for their plight. If he had turned against them he would have turned against a part of himself; he would have played the part of the Europeans, who disliked these misfits of their own creation. Furthermore, he would have risked assassination, which came to some of the older Kikuyu who supported the Government. Instead, Kenyatta tried at first to use this turbulent force to further his plans. It is probable that he hoped, not unreasonably, that if words could not penetrate the stiff white shirtfront of Government complacence, then a few outbursts of violence might do it. There were plenty of historical examples to support the view that force is the only language understood by dictatorship, even benevolent dictatorship.

But the only way that he could harness the desperate energy of these men was to show them results. For a time they would be satisfied with the excitement of shouting defiance of the Government at political meetings, but this was just a short-term drug and could have no lasting effect. The first oaths of Mau Mau were oaths of complicity and unity, directed against the Government and the European. It was not until shortly before Kenyatta's arrest in 1952 that the killing oath appeared. No move was made by London to break the deadlock, and it became only a matter of time before these men, in their own tormented way, broke out against unbearable oppression, as Irishmen, Hungarians, Russians, Americans, Frenchmen, and countless other peoples had done before them. At first Jomo Kenyatta certainly knew about their activities, although there is some evidence that he quite soon lost any really effective control over them. Once they had felt their own cruelly perverted strength, killing became a common bond of brotherhood which had its own momentum. Their hate-twisted souls serve as a tragic warning by human nature that if brotherhood is denied man in daylight, he will find it in darkness. To accuse Kenyatta of failing to avert this tragedy is to ignore the realities of a situation which can only too easily develop again in other parts of Africa.

Largely ignorant of the abyss towards which Kenya was moving, the settlers had been active in Kenya during these years in other ways. Between the end of the war and 1948, eight thousand new settlers had arrived to take up vacant areas in the White Highlands. Many of them had fought in the war as officers and had decided to leave England, with its Socialist rule and its restrictions, and seek an open-air life, free from the economic and political stresses of Europe. Unknown to them, they were coming to an economic and political tangle which made England appear by comparison a sane and prosperous paradise. Frightened that socialism might extend its grasp to the White Highlands, the settlers had formed a Kenya Plan which they sent to the British Government in 1949, proposing "the creation of a new British East Africa Dominion under European leadership." However, the liberalism of the Labour party was not so exhausted that it was taken in by the move. In the injudicious words of one settler: "Those who really know the

European position in Kenya consider that we possess today as much power and authority as we have ever had. But we cannot rest content with this." Alarmed by yet another move to extend white rule for ever, a counterpetition signed by nine African "Loyal Subjects" was sent to the King. After quoting a remark made by the Prime Minister of Britain, Clement Attlee, in his earliest years, to the effect that claims to self-government by white colonial minorities were "false demands," the petition concluded: "The long silence of the Africans in East and Central Africa has unfortunately led the English people . . . to paint and repaint a wrong picture of our Motherland. In the process of splashing paint over our land they have coated her with foreign names such as: . . . 'Colony,' 'Protectorate,' and now, 'Dominion.' The Europeans have done all this behind our back. What we really think and want is yet unexplored."

Underlining and aggravating the political wants were those which sprang from economic pressures. As always the land problem was in the forefront. Trade unionism was permitted but neither officially helped nor given encouragement by employers. Wages stayed at a minimum level. One of the real benefits of colonization, medicine, had permitted a sharp rise in the Kikuyu population, and in the Kiambu district near Nairobi it was officially estimated that nearly half the population would soon be without land, "something which cannot be faced with equanimity." Bordering on this district were large European farms and estates. The coffee crop was still virtually a monopoly of the Europeans. Terracing was still hampered by fears that as soon as the land was terraced the Europeans would take it. Taxation without representation was the policy for Africans. According to the U.N. Special Survey of 1953 the average annual income of the races in Kenya was Africans, 27 pounds; Asians, 280 pounds; Europeans, 660 pounds. In a parliamentary reply in the House of Commons as late as 1954 it was stated that the annual sum spent on primary education in Kenya was divided as follows: European child, £49 6s.; Asian child, 18s. 4d.; African child, 3s. As in Victorian England, Kenya was run primarily for the benefit of the rich, who were also white.

Despite the fact that from the beginning Jomo Kenyatta was strongly critical of Government policy, he neither could nor wanted to cut himself off completely from the European community. He had spent most of his adult life with Europeans and in some ways was closer to them than to his own people. His daughter Margaret told me that he once said to her, "The English are a wonderful people to live with, in England." His brother James, who has kept out of politics, told me that he never heard Jomo Kenyatta say he hated Europeans. "Sometimes he said he was happier with them than with ordinary people," he said, "and felt sad sometimes not to be back in England." James added that he did not believe Mau Mau ever had a proper leadership: "It spread like a fire."

A Scottish missionary considers that Kenyatta's attitude to religion then was "purely objective," and that he had tried, unsuccessfully, to get the Christian backing of the churches for his political plans. Until 1948 this missionary was frequently invited to open political meetings at Githunguri with prayers. "Things heated up a bit after that," he said, "and contact stopped." I asked whether he thought Kenyatta had led Mau Mau. "It is quite clear," he said, "that he accepted a certain amount of bloodshed as necessary, but I am also sure he made some attempt to stop it. I don't believe for a moment that Kenyatta organized Mau

Mau. My impression was that by 1952 he had largely lost control, and that to some extent things had ceased to matter for him."

An attempt at racial co-operation, which petered out into nothing, was made in mid-1950 when Kenyatta and Peter Koinange, the man who had started the college at Githunguri, approached some of the leading liberals among the Europeans in Nairobi and expressed their fears about the sharp deterioration in race relations. It was agreed to form a Kenya Citizens' Association, which had as its object the "fostering of better human relations in Kenya." The Governor gave it his blessing in a letter to the chairman and even said that it "must concern itself without hesitation or reserve with political questions." But the Association was doomed from the start. Apart from S. V. Cooke, who as usual realised the urgent need to solve the big issues quickly, most of the non-African members of the committee were infected by the same vapid liberalism which was all that the strains of war seemed to have left in the British mentality. They wanted to discuss African housing, and the low standard of African newspapers.

Almost as if they sensed, despite themselves, that this was a mere fiddling while Kenya burned, enthusiasm waned and after two whole years of occasional committee meetings the Association petered out. Human relations in Kenya, meanwhile, had reached a new low. For Kenyatta, conscious as he was of the cracks which were appearing all round him in the social fabric, this must have been just one more proof of the unlikelihood that Kenya could expect salvation from any move by the Europeans. No wonder a Kikuyu who has just emerged after seven years' detention for alleged complicity in Mau Mau told me: "No one knows if Kenyatta would have co-operated or not with the

Government. No single European co-operated with him because he was completely against imperialism. They should have given him a chance to show himself" — a slight exaggeration but not far from the truth.

There were, however, one or two Europeans who tried hard to come to terms with an increasingly complex situation. One of them was a civil servant with a very independent personality. He told me how he had attended the first joint meeting of European and African civil servants in Nairobi, and that the Africans had been so delighted at this rare co-operation that they had asked him to help in the political organization of K.A.U. The Government had wisely allowed him to accept the invitation and he had thereby come to see Kenyatta in action at committee meetings. "He would sit like a chief at the end of the table," he said, "while the others made their speeches, and then he told them what to do. He was an intuitive and spiritual person, although far too cynical to think of himself as a second Christ . . . The situation then was exceedingly aggravating for an African, and he went mad in an African way. I don't blame him; I'd have done the same . . . Jomo had an amazing sweep of vision, and felt his beliefs passionately. I think he was one of the most positive and alive people I have met . . . I do very greatly admire him and I share with him the belief that some things have to be destroyed before they can be built up."

But for the majority of Kenya Europeans the name of Jomo Kenyatta aroused anger and fear. Earlier moves by the settlers to have him deported for that crime beloved by all insecure rulers, subversion, had been thwarted by the Government. Farmers looked at their simple farm workers, usually the only type of African they had ever met, and laughed at the idea that they should want to run a modern state on their own. Most never realised that domination by foreigners could cripple even a simple peasant mind, and, by removing initiative, could impose a subtle form of slavery.

Another name which aroused almost as much irritation in the minds of the settlers as Kenyatta's was that of an English Labour M.P., Fenner Brockway. His only sin was that he had a consistent record of anti-colonialism and tended to treat Africans with more respect than settlers. In 1950 he paid a visit to Kenya, and called on Jomo Kenyatta, whom he had known in London. "He seemed unchanged," he writes; "aquiline features, tall, a cloak over his shoulders, an ivory-topped stick in his hand, sometimes smiling radiantly, sometimes severe, a fascinating showman." Fenner Brockway stayed at the house of the late ex-Senior Chief Koinange, who died in 1960 very shortly after his release from detention, aged ninety. He was the father of Peter Koinange, the teacher, and the family became the object of Government suspicion before and during Mau Mau. They lived close to the White Highlands and claimed that some of their land had been taken by the Europeans. Another strong grievance was that they had not been allowed to grow coffee, which was earning for the settlers sky-high prices at that time.

The ex-Senior Chief, a small man with a quiet voice and great dignity, explained his feelings to Fenner Brockway in simple terms: "When someone steals your ox, it is killed and roasted and eaten. One can forget. When someone steals your land, especially if nearby, one can never forget. It is always there . . ." Together with Peter Koinange and Kenyatta, the ex-Senior Chief and Fenner Brockway discussed the possibilities of constitutional advance and the supply of information concerning Kenya's problems to the

House of Commons. Fenner Brockway wrote of Kenyatta: "He gave every evidence of sincerity and must have been an extremely good actor if he was misleading us." Kenyatta was an extremely good actor, but he had everything to gain by winning his objectives peacefully. He was far too intelligent not to know that if the thug element in his following took the lead the resultant chaos would ruin his plans for an independent viable African society.

Fenner Brockway discussed with Kenyatta the status of Kikuyu women, who have to carry immense loads of firewood on their backs, and appear to the outsider to lead a miserable existence. Kenyatta said that another Englishman had once asked him this. "I asked him where his wife was," chuckled Jomo. "She was putting clothes through a mangle in the kitchen, as hard work as carrying firewood on your back."[1] But he agreed that changes would come with education and political and social freedom. At Kenyatta's house in Githunguri they discussed books. "Jomo was proud of his library," wrote Fenner Brockway, "and as he took one after another from his shelves and pressed them back he spoke with a genuine love of his books. I liked him more at this moment than I had ever done."[2]

Their political discussions ranged over land hunger, the "squatters," low wages, African representation, European domination, and the need for K.A.U. to win the support of the other tribes. "Not once," wrote Fenner Brockway, "did he give a hint that he was contemplating anything beyond accepted political organization and activity . . . never in one phrase did he suggest that he foresaw, much less planned, the violence and atrocities of Mau Mau." Again, it is unlikely that a revolutionary would confide such plans to a comparative stranger, but there was still a dim possi-

[1] *African Journeys*, Fenner Brockway, p. 94.   [2] *Ibid.*, p. 96.

bility that changes would be made which would disarm the extremists.

In a farewell speech at a large multiracial tea party given by the ex-Senior Chief, Fenner Brockway spoke about human rights and democracy, but he records that it was the following phrase which won a storm of applause: "When a baby is born, it is not the pigment of the skin which makes it precious; it is the life, the spirit, within that little form, be it white, brown or black, which makes it sacred."[3] Sentimental? Perhaps, to people born into a free society, but in Kenya it touched the very core of African politics. Before leaving, Fenner Brockway accompanied Kenyatta to a political meeting in Nairobi. There were six hundred inside the hall and about six thousand outside. The usual political points were made, and Kenyatta excitedly waved to the dense crowds as he drove off, like a king among royalists.

An Indian who has played an important part in Kenya politics told me that at another meeting in Nairobi he noticed a new element in Kenyatta's reception. "As he appeared in the hall people stood up in thousands, in reverence, as one would expect royalty to be treated . . . there was something new in his relationship with the masses and he had become more than just a political leader." The same Indian added that although Kenyatta's dominance over the people appeared to be "absolute," he "sometimes seemed to have a bitterness in his heart — a hopelessness at the chances of breaking through the political opposition which faced him . . . He later got swept away on the tide."

The Kenya Government was suffering from a curious paralysis. Its eyes followed the movements around it, and the lips parted, but little sound was heard and there was

[3] *Ibid.*, p. 109.

scarcely a twitch from the limbs. The official Corfield Report on Mau Mau (1960), which has all the peculiar interest of a case-history composed by the patient himself, is also a reliable chronicle of Government information at this time.

From police informers scattered through the Kikuyu Reserve came reports of secret oathing ceremonies, with all the weird and magical paraphernalia which accompanied them. Sheep's eyes, banana leaves, and dead cats were among the tools of the oath administrator. Later, as this social madness became more pronounced, the oaths became a more and more obscene travesty of the traditional Kikuyu oaths. They were held at night in isolated huts, and the fear-crazed administrators conducted almost unimaginable sexual orgies involving menstrual blood and the organs of sheep. It was a nightmare of the human spirit which had a strange parallel in Europe between the middle of the thirteenth and the end of the seventeenth centuries, when black magic became a refuge for some of those who had lost their Christian faith. Hundreds of thousands of people were put to death at that period in Western Europe for alleged witchcraft.

The same symptoms were there: midnight meetings, obscene songs and dances, sexual orgies, weird reversals of the traditional beliefs, and homage to the Devil. Writing of this phenomenon, the former Kenya Government psychiatrist, Dr. J. C. Carothers, says: "It seems that the one thing that all these people had in common was a desire to achieve some personal aim which they could not achieve within the 'righteous' social framework of their time."[4] As the undisputed political leader of the Kikuyu tribe, Jomo Kenyatta was awarded, willy-nilly, the post of the Devil in

[4] *The Psychology of Mau Mau*, Dr. J. C. Carothers, 1955, p. 15.

these incantations. Striving to find expression, the religious spirit of the Kikuyu clung to the magnetic personality of Jomo Kenyatta, not only in the debased form of Mau Mau, but also within that still relatively normal part of the tribe, which began to substitute his name in hymns for that of Christ. This shocked many Europeans, but their shock was at least partly unjustified. Nationalism, particularly in Africa, is a religious as well as a political force. Much of its dynamic energy derives from a spiritual need to escape from that domination of foreign dogma. In Ghana (then called the Gold Coast) Nkrumah's name had been used likewise by the more militant nationalists.

British justice in Kenya pursued its lumbering and meticulous course, quite unable to cope adequately with this social perversion. "There can be no doubt," said a magistrate when convicting a group of oath administrators, "that the nineteen accused, some of whom are partially educated, have reverted to, or still are, in no better mental or moral state than the African in the days of Livingstone. . . ."[5] This essentially moralistic and mistaken idea that Mau Mau was simply a reversion to type became the typical European reaction to Mau Mau. To think of Mau Mau as a social disease, which it was, would have transferred much of the blame for it to the leaders of Kenya's society, and they came near to washing their hands of the whole affair, as is borne out by the Corfield Report itself. According to Mr. Corfield, Mau Mau was caused primarily by Jomo Kenyatta, and secondarily by the Government's inadequate intelligence system. In his eyes, those of an administrator with many years' service administering colonials in Africa, the disastrous failure of the Government to explore the wishes and the wants of the Africans, and the pernicious

[5] Corfield Report, p. 86.

colour bar, were little more than inevitable strains in a society in transition.

On August 4, 1950, Mau Mau was declared an illegal society, although nobody knew for certain who was behind it, if anyone. At about the same time Government officials were hearing rumours that a campaign of civil disobedience was being planned.[6] K.A.U. itself was undergoing strains and stresses. Jomo Kenyatta was having to control a wide range of opinion, ranging from men who made no secret of their allegiance to Mau Mau and violence, and others who still hoped to gain independence by asking for it. Among the latter were some staunch Christians whose faith had a sobering effect on their political needs. Their newly won spiritual self-confidence, however, sustained a terrible hammering in these days and many succumbed for want of encouragement from a society which tended to lock up its religion in church.

Towards the end of the year a police report from one Kikuyu district ran:

"It is said that the tension is growing, and a political consciousness with an evil outlook is already present among a dangerous portion of the tribe. Whilst it is considered that the Kikuyu leaders of today will never associate themselves with major disturbances, it is insisted that their policy is one of cunning and secretive provocation — promoting ill-will against Government and the European community whenever possible, and aiming for the day when they can 'innocently' declare themselves unable to control the fury of their followers and take a back seat whilst their flock engage in violent anti-Government activity. It is submitted that the day-to-day manner of the average individual Kikuyu, while presenting a normal exterior, gives a

[6] *Ibid.*, p. 90.

false impression of his state of mind, and that not until he
sees his fellow Africans in numbers at a meeting, where he
feels there is security against Government intervention,
does he voice his thoughts and disclose his true political
attitude."[7]

This report was probably an extremely accurate one, if
judged against the true background facts. Failure to advance by constitutional means had inevitably swung the
nationalist energy towards violence. The leaders, Kenyatta
included, probably hoped that a minor breakdown in law
and order might wake up the British Government to the
urgency of drastic reform. However, they were not dealing
with the disciplined modern gangsters of an EOKA movement, but with the only form of African violence possible
in Kenya, night-time attacks with pangas. A lack of discipline quickly resulted in an uncontrolled spread of violence of a peculiarly brutal kind.

The so-called two-faced nature of the Kikuyu has often
been remarked on. Servants who smiled happily during the
day sometimes attacked their employers at night. Office
clerks who worked quietly and obediently for their firms
became mad with excitement at political meetings. Sometimes respected church leaders were found to have organized Mau Mau ceremonies during the night. Jomo Kenyatta himself is accused of having said one thing and meant
another. There is an explanation for this which seldom
seems to be recognized. Being an unusually intelligent and
quick-witted people, the Kikuyu found they could act two
parts with ease. The acting was forced upon them by circumstances. Their first reaction to the European had been
one of wonder and almost awe, and they quickly decided
they would adopt many of the new ways offered to them.

[7] *Ibid.*, p. 98.

However, they became caught in midstream, with the promise of the new civilization, but not its fulfillment. For a time they could maintain this balance between two worlds with difficulty. The exterior self became the one which they wanted to be, and the one the European wanted to see, and the other self was that part which still belonged to the old order. For those who found the way forward blocked by the racial colour bar, with its attendant evils, there was only one course open in the end — retreat. The smile became left behind in mid-air, with no body, like that of the Cheshire cat. Sharing as he did the whole range of Kikuyu feeling, Jomo Kenyatta would have been betraying himself as well as his followers if he had spurned those who wanted his leadership, even those who were being sucked into the awful abyss of Mau Mau. It was not a question of right or wrong, but of a natural compulsion to survive as a person and as a people.

As the months of 1951 dragged past and the political situation deteriorated, the African idea of freedom, which not long before had included equal rights with Europeans, crystallized into a simple desire to expel all Europeans from Kenya. A typical oathing ceremony took place on a settler's farm on February 3, and six men were arrested and imprisoned. In a comment sent to the Member for Law and Order, the Director of Intelligence and Security said: "The name of Jomo Kenyatta is frequently mentioned as a super-human who will guide the African towards freedom and remove the European from the Colony."[8]

It is worth observing at this point how curiously inconsistent was the behaviour of the Kenya Government during this time. In simple terms of law and order they were well aware that an ugly situation was developing. They also

[8] *Ibid.*, p. 105.

knew that Jomo Kenyatta and some others were regarded by the malcontents as their leaders. There can be few governments in the world which would not have promptly put them in prison, with or without a trial, and hoped that the trouble would disappear with the leaders. But the Kenya Government could not act like a tin-pot dictatorship for the very good reason that it justified its existence, in its own eyes as well as in the eyes of the world, by its "civilizing mission." In the words of its then Governor, Sir Philip Mitchell, its task was to "civilise a great mass of human beings who are at present in a very primitive moral, cultural and social state, albeit most of them are eager to go further."[9] The Kenya Government could only lock people up without trial at the expense of its conscience and its reputation. On the other hand, it lacked the energy and the conviction to put into practise the ideals which had created the most worth-while parts of Western civilization. It knew its part but was too paralyzed to act it out. The result was a feeble liberalism which permitted a certain amount of free speech and hesitated before brutal repression. There was plenty of honest administrative energy within the Government, but it was perishing for want of vision, which alone could have inspired it to rise to the formidable task of statesmanship demanded of it.

But it would be inaccurate to put all the blame on this imaginatively tired Government. The source of the lethargy was not in Kenya but in London itself. This became evident with the visit to Kenya in May 1951 of the Colonial Secretary, James Griffiths. The British Government then was a Labour Government, and in no political group in England was there a greater desire to give political free-

---

[9] A dispatch from Sir Philip to the Secretary of State for the Colonies concerning Local Government in Kenya.

dom to colonial peoples than in the Labour party. James Griffiths himself was a man who had risen from a humble background in South Wales. As a former miner in the days of economic depression he must have known very well what it was like to fight for elementary social and economic rights. In his visit it seemed as if the gods were offering a last-minute opportunity for Kenya to escape the impending storm. If he had had the imagination and courage to push through drastic political and economic reforms the situation might have been saved. His failure to do so was a personal political failure of the first magnitude, but it was also a failure of Labour leadership in England, and thus marked the near eclipse of one of Britain's finest gifts to the world — her radical tradition. Events since have done little to qualify this impression.

Frenzied political activity by K.A.U. heralded the Colonial Secretary's arrival. A memorandum was drawn up, to be presented by Jomo Kenyatta. As James Griffiths' arrival followed an announcement in London that constitutional changes were planned for Kenya, the excitement was understandable. The memorandum contained demands for twelve elected African members instead of the then four nominated members who had to represent the interests of five million people; abolition of the colour bar; Government aid for African farmers; and greater freedom for trade unions.

The District Commissioner of the Nyeri district said in a secret report on a K.A.U. meeting held at the end of the Colonial Secretary's visit: "It was clearly stated that the Secretary of State would be given a period to accede to their requests, but that if the answer was unfavourable, other methods would have to be employed." In fact the immediate interim proposals were that 40,000 Europeans were to have fourteen elected members, 100,000 Indians were to have six, 24,000 Arabs were to have one, and 5 million Africans were to have five nominated members. There would be twenty-six official members to support Government policy.

One extra nominated member as an answer to the African demands was about as effective as throwing a ham sandwich to a famished lion. The Colonial Secretary had made the mistake of his life. The only people who were pleased with his visit were the settlers, who had asked for parity of representation with all the other unofficial members combined and found to their delight that they still had a majority.

One after another the safety valves had been bolted down, and now there was nothing to do but wait for the explosion. But it was not until exactly a year later that the killing oath and the Mau Mau murder campaign began. One by one the Kikuyu people were willingly or forcibly taking the Mau Mau oath. Meanwhile, for the settlers, the sundowners, the cricket matches, the farming, and the holidays by Kenya's beautiful coast, went on as usual, although one or two were becoming alarmed. Even the Government was not aware that anything really serious was about to happen. Jomo Kenyatta continued to address enormous meetings, and continued from time to time to obey Government requests for denunciations of Mau Mau — denunciations which did not convince the Government, and, for reasons already stated, probably did not carry very much conviction to anyone, including himself. The time when reasoned political thinking could succeed was past. In a letter to the Provincial Commissioner of the Kikuyu area, written on June 21, 1951, the District Commissioner of Nyeri district described the deteriorating situation and said: ". . . the hatred of the young men from Nairobi is something that can be felt whenever one meets them in the reserve." Demonstrating the estrangement of the head of Government from the feet, a report appeared in the *Kenya Weekly News* (a settler paper) of March 14, 1952, saying: "Speaking in London last month, His Excellency the Governor said that the general political feeling in Kenya was better than he had ever known it for many years, a statement which must have surprised many who read it."

On July 26 a meeting of K.A.U. took place at the small town of Nyeri, which lies in the shadow of Mount Kenya. It was to be one of the last political meetings held in Kenya for some years. The District Commissioner saw it in the following way:

Over 20,000 men, women and children attended. K.A.U. insinuated over forty bus loads of Nairobi thugs and prostitutes, who were clearly under instructions to excite the crowd. The buses arrived with Mau Mau grass ringlets bedecking their bonnets, and beneath the K.A.U. flag was to be seen the complete paraphernalia of Mau Mau. The speakers, Jomo Kenyatta, Ochieng, and Kaggia, followed the hackneyed lines of attack, the former soft-pedalling noticeably and the latter in vociferous strain.

Many of the vast crowd heard nothing of the proceedings, though the thugs weaving through it announced that the day of action had arrived; the atmosphere was tense and the crowd afraid of itself. It was noticeable that Jomo Kenyatta himself, from the rostrum, took ten minutes to restore control after an excellent and balanced pro-Government speech by Senior Chief Nderi. A spokesman, under official instructions, received a completely non-committal reply from Jomo when he asked him what steps he (Jomo) would take to stamp out Mau Mau.

A full report was made of the meeting by a police officer, and some extracts from Jomo Kenyatta's speech may help to indicate the kind of ideas he expressed in public at this time, only three months before his arrest and the declaration of a State of Emergency. He begins:

I am very pleased to come to Nyeri and see so many of you here at this meeting of K.A.U., but before we open the meeting, I appeal to you to sit down and keep quiet so that you can hear what we are going to say. [Considerable shouting and excitement among the crowd nearly drowned his words.] . . . Those who are continuing to make a noise must be removed from this meeting. I do not want any interruptions. I am the leader of Mumbi and I ask you yet again to keep quiet. [Tremendous applause and the crowd becomes more orderly.] What God has told me to say to you today I will now say . . . You are the earth and the earth is ours so listen to me and don't interrupt any more. . . .

There followed some short prayers from an African minister, which are themselves interesting. "Those who are despised," says the minister, "are those who fight for freedom. God said that one man cannot knock down a wall and continue to freedom, but if people unite and push together they could break the wall and pass over the ground to independence. May God be with us on this day. We are here to follow the principles of justice. May God lead us on to our goal. Jomo is a disciple of God who will lead you along the righteous path. In the name of Jesus Christ and the people of Mumbi, I give you my blessing." This mixture of religion and politics probably expressed the feeling of the great mass of the Kikuyu people of this time. At one extreme were the few who followed the European belief that politics should not be linked with religion, and at the

other extreme were the lost men of the Mau Mau for whom
both religion and politics had become subordinated to a
blind submission to violence.

Jomo Kenyatta then continues, after a long-drawn cry
of "eeeeee," which always heralded his speeches and always won delighted applause. Sweat standing out on his
forehead in the midday heat, this consummate actor now
has what he always loved, the attention of an audience of
many thousands.

. . . I want you to know the purpose of K.A.U. It is the
biggest purpose the African has. It involves every African
in Kenya and it is their mouthpiece which asks for freedom. [Applause] If we unite now, each and every one of
us, and each tribe to another, we will cause the implemen-
tation in this country of that which the European calls
democracy. True democracy has no colour distinction. It
does not choose between black and white. We are here in
this tremendous gathering under the K.A.U. flag to find
which road leads us from darkness into democracy. In
order to find it we Africans must first achieve the right to
elect our own representatives in the Legislature and we are
going to set about to rectify this situation. [Applause] We
feel we are dominated by a handful of others who refuse
to be just. [Applause] . . . God said this is our land. Land
in which we are to flourish as a people. We are not worried
that other races are here with us in our country, but we
insist that we are the leaders here, and what we want we
insist we get. We want our cattle to get fat on our land so
that our children grow up in prosperity; we do not want
that fat removed to feed others. [Applause] He who has
ears should now hear that K.A.U. claims this land as its
own gift from God and I wish those who are black, white
or brown at this meeting to know this. K.A.U. speaks in
daylight. He who calls us the Mau Mau is not truthful. We
do not know this thing called Mau Mau. [Jeers and ap-
plause] We want to prosper as a nation, and as a nation

we demand equality ... It has never been known in history that a nation prospers without equality . . . As long as people are held down, corruption is sure to rise and the only answer to this is a policy of equality. . . .

Our country today is in a bad state for it is a land full of fools — and fools in a country delay the independence of its people. K.A.U. seeks to remedy this situation, and I tell you now it despises thieving, robbery and murder for these practises ruin our country . . . Those people are wrecking our chances of advancement . . . If I have my own way, let me tell you I would butcher the criminal, and there are more criminals than one in more senses than one. The policeman must arrest an offender . . . but he must not go about picking up people with a small horn of liquor in their hands and march them in procession with his fellow policemen to Government and say he has got a Mau Mau amongst the Kikuyu people. [Applause] The plainclothes man who hides in the hedges must, I demand, get the truth of our words before he flies to Government to present them with false information.

Kenyatta then lets loose some more caustic comments about those who acted as Government informers. Tremendous cheers greet his remarks and the crowd shows signs of getting out of hand. The police officer present tells Kenyatta that unless he can bring the crowd under control he must not make any more "racial remarks." Jomo Kenyatta agrees and spends fifteen minutes moving about among the crowd and quietening them.

He then goes on to discuss land, and he asks who among the crowd want more land. Each person raises both hands. "Who do not want more land?" Nobody moved. "I think the Europeans here realize in their heart of hearts that our grievance is true. [Shouts of "What are they going to do about it?"] "Who of you are going to support K.A.U.?" [All raise their hands and there is tremendous applause.]

"Is it your heart that supports the K.A.U. or is it merely your mouth?" [Answer, "Our hearts," and the crowd rises to its feet in excitement. Seven minutes pass before calm is restored.] "Then join us today in this union of ours. Do not be scared of the few policemen under those trees who are holding their rifles high in the air for you to see. Their job is to seize criminals and we shall save them a job today." Kenyatta then makes an appeal for money, and a collection is made. The K.A.U. flag is hoisted at this stage, above the platform, and beneath it is tied a piece of sugar cane: sugar cane is used in Mau Mau ceremonies, and its appearance now is greeted with cheers.

Jomo Kenyatta then warns against the dangers of drink, saying that beer makes fools and criminals. He is interrupted by shouts that the crowd wants to hear about land, not beer, and once more uproar follows. The police officer, who is seated by the platform, describes the confusion with difficulty: "Whereas before there were a few feet of space between us and the crowd, we are now swamped with wriggling masses, one of whom is even sitting on the back of the chair on which I am sitting." The policeman's lot at that time was indeed not a happy one. An African Government officer then tries to speak, and he asks what Kenyatta plans to do to stop Mau Mau. He has to leave the platform, however, when the crowd shouts him down. Jomo Kenyatta then goes on to say that K.A.U. is "not a fighting union that uses fists and weapons . . . remember the old saying that he who hits with a rungu returns, but he who is hit with justice never comes back," and he refers disparagingly to "so-called" Mau Mau. Senior Chief Nderi (soon afterwards to be murdered by Mau Mau) then tries to put the Government case. "Nobody but Government can help us," he says. Terrific and prolonged jeers and booing follow and he has to stand down. "The mood of the meeting is bad," writes the police officer, "and I personally feel that all that remains is for the cooking pot to be brought on."

At this moment a company of armoured cars passes by on its way to a military exercise, and the sight of them sobers the crowd somewhat. Kenyatta then asks the crowd not to be "cross" with the Senior Chief, in a rather don't-shoot-the-pianist-he-is-doing-his-best manner. There follows a hard-hitting speech from an able young Luo called Ochieng Oneko. "We have seen for too long," he says, "that the European gets first place . . . We want co-operation and friendship between races but we do not want that friendship that resembles the friendship of the crocodile and the fish . . . Europeans are visitors and they know it . . . They have to give us permission before we can go to the lavatory. If we want freedom we must hit back. I know we will get it. We will get it in the same way as the people in the Gold Coast and Nigeria . . . Regarding religion. We do not know God. What we know is Ngai. We believe in Ngai whether the missionaries say we are pagans or not. Are we not led by the God of Africa . . . If you do not unite, you will be the person who is kicked in the backside and called 'Boy' . . . Those who came to this country to eke out a living when they were kicked out of India will repeat the performance of evacuation in time. . . ." There is a fresh wave of uproar as he sits down.

After this burst of verbal high explosive Kenyatta ends the meeting with a few more words. He describes the K.A.U. flag to the crowd. "Black is to show that this is for black people," he says; "red is to show that the blood of an African is the same colour as the blood of a European, and green is to show that when we were given this country by God it was green, fertile, and good, but now you see the green is below the red and is suppressed." [Tremendous applause] He explains that the shield and the spear and the arrow on the flag do not indicate that they should fight like their fathers. "What could a spear do against an atom bomb? The weapon with which we will fight is justice and brains." After a hymn, in which Jomo Kenyatta is praised as a disciple of God, the meeting breaks up peacefully.

However, communication between subjects and rulers in Kenya was so tenuous that neither the just anger of this meeting nor its dangerous passion was fully noted by the Government. Although the Government was increasingly perturbed by the growing lawlessness it was with the greatest reluctance that it admitted anything serious was wrong. This typical British calm, or blindness to the facts, is exemplified by the opening sentence of the official *Colonial Office Report on the Colony and Protectorate of Kenya for the year 1952*, the year in which a State of Emergency was declared and Mau Mau began its killing in earnest. "Of all the events of the year," writes the author, "the most memorable is the visit to the Colony of Her Majesty the Queen (then Her Royal Highness the Princess Elizabeth) and His Royal Highness the Duke of Edinburgh . . . They visited the Pumwani Maternity Hospital and attended a Garden Party at Government House. . . ."

Shortly before the Nyeri meeting the Governor, Sir Philip Mitchell, retired, and it was not until the end of September that the new Governor, Sir Evelyn Baring, arrived. Meanwhile, on August 17 the Acting Governor warned the Colonial Office in London that there was trouble ahead. In the course of his letter he described Mau Mau as being the "covert organization" behind K.A.U., and added, "there need be little doubt, though there is no proof, that he [Kenyatta] controls this revolutionary organization in so far as it is still susceptible to control. . . ." As late as the end of September there was still no proof in the hands of the Government that Kenyatta was the organizer of Mau Mau, despite the fact that for at least three years the Kenya Police had been watching his every move with the aid of hundreds of informers. In a report submitted to the new Governor on October 4 by the Chief Native Commissioner it was stated: "Although there is no direct evidence to prove Kenyatta's connection with Mau Mau, a number of factors point to his close association with this society."

By this time the forces of violence were beginning to erupt throughout Kikuyuland. Cattle on European farms were hamstrung and disembowelled. Bodies of brutally murdered Africans were discovered in Kikuyu villages, killed because they had objected to taking the oaths, or because they were Government officials. A widely respected Kikuyu, Senior Chief Waruhiu, was murdered in Chicago style near his home on October 7, in broad daylight: he was shot by gangsters who had forced his car into the side of the road. He was a staunch Christian, and a Government employee. The Member for Law and Order himself had a personal bodyguard, having received a threatening letter — a symbolic example of the collapse of that once so proud and confident "civilizing mission." However, although the new Governor, a man of great administrative ability, quickly saw the need to restore law and order by an urgent reinforcement of security measures, he showed very little awareness of the terrible sense of oppression felt by the Kikuyu people.

At 5 P.M. on October 20, 1952, the Governor signed the proclamation declaring a State of Emergency, and orders were immediately signed authorizing the detention of 183 Africans. Jomo Kenyatta was one of them, and that evening he was arrested and flown in a police aircraft to the remote Northern Frontier District, where he was to remain for the next years of his life.

The young man with the passionate convictions and shaky self-confidence who had visited England twenty-three years earlier to represent his tribe had later become the equally passionate and histrionic student of anthropology, but with new self-assurance encouraged by his obvious ability. Then came the return home, the excitement of full-time politics, and the hope of political freedom, to be followed by a long and increasingly bitter struggle against the tyranny of good intentions offered by the Kenya Government. Finally, exactly fifty years since white settlement in Kenya began, the most outstanding leader in the colony was arrested. In the eyes of the Government and the settlers he had become a devil, and in the eyes of the Africans he had become a god. While English soldiers, Kenya settlers, and Mau Mau terrorists fought out their long gruesome battle under the blind stare of Mount Kenya, the myth of Kenyatta was to dominate the shaping of Kenya politics, as his magnetic presence had dominated the thousands who heard him. The bullets, the pangas, and the 13,547 corpses were to achieve nothing final, but merely postpone the day when both black and white would have to find, for their own peace of mind, a rational answer to the two-headed myth of their own creation.

Some words spoken by Sir Philip Mitchell in Kenya's Legislative Council, shortly before his retirement, can serve as a sadly ironic epilogue to these miserable few years. "Exacted obedience," he said, "is always a negative thing; it promotes a sterile condition in which there is no disorder — but it can neither create nor give scope to those creative and productive forces on which the progress of communities depends . . . There is neither place nor opportunity for dissent or opposition; the only choice is between acquiescence or agitation, subservience or sedition." The Kenya Government knew how to swim, and yet it was drowning.

CHAPTER TEN

THE QUEEN AGAINST KENYATTA

ON THE night that Jomo Kenyatta and many of his associates were arrested and a State of Emergency declared, military reinforcements began to arrive in the colony. A regiment of British soldiers was flown from the frying pan of the terrorist-ridden Suez Canal Zone into the spreading fire of Kenya. The Kenya Regiment (composed of European settlers) was called up. Units of the King's African Rifles arrived from neighbouring Tanganyika and Uganda. The cruiser H.M.S. *Kenya* sailed into Mombasa harbour, although it is doubtful if the crew knew why. Perhaps the chair-borne admirals in London had not been told that three hundred miles of solid Africa separated the Indian Ocean from the Kikuyu Reserve.

After half a century of colonial rule Britain's latest answer to the testing problems which faced her in Kenya was a display of military force. The psychological chaos of the Kikuyu was to be met now by methods directly descended from the primitive mind of Genghis Khan, owing little to the ideals of Western liberalism, which had been the creative part of the "civilizing mission."

In Nairobi settlers began to buy revolvers, shotguns, and sirens, with which to defend their isolated farms. One week after the emergency was declared a settler was hacked to death — the first white victim of Mau Mau. The scene was now set for the next few years — years during which most Europeans looked on each African as a potential murderer, and when each European became a symbol of oppression in the eyes of most Africans. The floating suspicions and fears of the past few years crystallized as hard racial antagonism.

But beneath the brisk new military efficiency was a lurking sense of shame at the way events had gone. This shame could be glibly explained away by criticism of the Government's poor use of its police force, but the explanation satisfied nothing except a dying myth — the defensive myth of racial supremacy. Evidence of this unexpressed feeling is seen in the incredible speed with which African political development moved during the next few years. There is no good mythological reason why it suddenly became "right and proper" to give African politicians as much as, and more than, Jomo Kenyatta had asked for during those dead years after the war. The Africans were still as "uncivilized." The only satisfactory explanation is that once again the British had demonstrated their unique capacity to drift into disaster and then extricate themselves with nonchalance, as if the whole affair had been carefully planned from the beginning. But this is to jump the gun. The myth may have been dying at this time, but it still had life in it. Someone must be to blame for the disaster of Mau Mau. As the scapegoat could not be a member of the myth, even an inefficient member like the Member for Law and Order, he must be an African. What worse African was there than Jomo Kenyatta? It was he who had been graciously "given" a Western education, and all the thanks he returned was to bite the hand of the myth which fed him. Jomo Kenyatta was almost unanimously chosen to fulfil the role of Devil.

However, the Kenya Government pursued its myth with

moderation, as was its habit, and refused to give way to some of the wilder demands that Kenyatta should be hanged out of hand for treason. Brutality was not "cricket," but "moral attitudes" could be. "You have much to answer for and for that you will be punished. The maximum sentences which this Court is empowered to pass are the sentences which I do pass, and I can only comment that in my opinion they are inadequate for what you have done." Thus the official voice of the myth, delivered with all the pompous finality of British justice by the Magistrate who tried Jomo Kenyatta.

But the mechanics of this justice had to be gone through before the appropriate decision was arrived at. One month after he was arrested Jomo Kenyatta was charged with managing Mau Mau, and being a member of it, since it was banned in 1950. Five of his associates, all of them leading members of K.A.U., were to be tried with him. One of them was a trade union leader, who had at one time attended a Moral Rearmament conference in Switzerland. Another was a political journalist. A third was an independent religious leader, and this man, Kaggia, had a significant background. He later described to the court how he had left school in 1939, and after working for his local District Commissioner as a clerk, had joined the army. He had risen to the rank of Quartermaster Sergeant before the war ended, when he became a religious reformer. Kaggia had been brought up as an Anglican, within the auspices of the Church Missionary Society, but during a visit to England he had seen something of the activities of the Church there, and had returned to Kenya determined to encourage changes. When asked to state what changes, he cited the colour bar, "which I strongly abhor and hate." Like Kenyatta, Kaggia claimed to be an "undenominational" Christian. When asked if he believed in violence as a political weapon, he replied, "No, all the time when I started my movement I have been a believer of non-violence and I still maintain that belief in my political activities because I could join the practice of Jesus Christ and that of Mahatma Gandhi which I consider as the two very good examples of Christianity and that is what I believe and practise."

During Kaggia's cross-examination there developed a perhaps symbolic duel on the meaning of Christ's teaching. Kaggia claimed that Christ taught about the rights of mankind, to which the Magistrate replied, "I put it to you that Jesus Christ stood more for the duties of humanity and human kind . . ." To which Kaggia retorted, "Don't you agree that he stood for both?" Even Christ became used as a witness for the prosecution.

But the trial was not intended to touch on such lofty matters. Understandably in the circumstances, the Kenya Government did all it could to damp down the intense interest engendered by the trial far beyond the borders of Kenya. "It is a criminal case," asserted the Crown Counsel at one point. ". . . It would have been the same if 'Queen against Kenyatta' were for a felony or picking a pocket; to describe it as a State Trial would invest it with a halo it does not really possess." However, the Crown Counsel's advice was not taken and the "halo" was duly bestowed on the trial by almost anyone with any interest in the fate of Africa.

Although the Government could not determine the attitude of the public, its physical control over this case ensured that it was held as far from the limelight as possible. It was decided that it should be held in the tiny administrative outpost of Kapenguria, on the western border of

Kenya, and nearly three hundred miles from Nairobi and possible demonstrations. Kapenguria was so little known, even to Government officials in Nairobi, that when a Resident Magistrate was chosen to hear the case he was appointed to the wrong province by mistake. There are no railways, hotels, or telephones at Kapenguria, and the only buildings of any note are those belonging to the local District Commissioner and a District Officer, and a prison and an agricultural school. The trial was held in the agricultural school.

The physical limitations of both the small courtroom and Kapenguria's lack of facilities caused considerable irritation to all concerned. Lawyers, magistrates, clerks and journalists, not to mention onlookers, had to live in the attractive little settler town of Kitale, twenty miles away, and drive through the choking dust of appalling roads to the court each day. To add to the difficulties of the African and Indian defense lawyers (the defence team included a Punjabi, a Sikh, a Goan, a Jamaican, a Nigerian, and D. N. Pritt, a well-known English Q.C.), the only hotel in Kitale was for Europeans only, so that when these men wanted to consult their leader, D. N. Pritt, they had to do it in a house belonging to an Indian businessman. They had a police guard because it was feared that local settlers might take the law into their own hands.

The trial began on November 24, after an objection by the Defence concerning the Magistrate had been turned down. He was a retired judge from Kenya's Supreme Court named Thacker, and it was claimed that as he had already tried a case in which one of the accused had narrowly escaped conviction for attempted murder, he would be biased. This was denied, and the case opened quietly. The Magistrate sat at what was usually the teacher's desk on a platform. Behind him on the wall was a coloured print of the Queen. Settlers filled the spectators' enclosure; the men with wide-brimmed hats, shorts, and revolvers, and the women with their knitting. Outside were strong detachments of police.

As the prisoners filed in and took their seats all eyes turned to look at Kenyatta, the centre of the drama. A European woman thought he looked rather ill, but otherwise self-assured. "Kenyatta's face," she wrote afterwards, "was composed, almost impassive. Dressed in brown corduroy trousers, a brown suede jacket zipped up the front, a russet-coloured shirt open at the neck, and a beaded belt, he seemed very self-possessed."[1] She also remarked on the hypnotic effect of his eyes. All the accused pleaded not guilty, and a short adjournment of a few days was allowed to give the leader of the Defence, D. N. Pritt, Q.C., time to arrive from England.

Kenya's Deputy Public Prosecutor opened the case with a brief definition of Mau Mau — a description which demonstrates the slightly unreal tone of the proceedings. The thought-forms of British law were to prove hardly less unsuccessful than the Government in seeking to get to grips with Africa. "May it please Your Honour," he began, ". . . I would ask your Honour to take notice of the prohibition of this society published in the *Gazette* of the Colony, and its effective date which is 12 August 1950. The dates between which the charges are set are 12th August 1950 and 21st October 1952 the date on which the accused, or at least five of them, ceased to be free agents . . .

"The Society is Mau Mau. It is a Society which has no records. It appears to have no official list of members. It does not carry banners. Some details of its meetings and its

[1] *In the Shadow of the Mau Mau*, Ione Leigh, p. 99.

rites, the instruments of which are got from the local bush, will be heard later in the proceedings. Arches of banana leaves, the African fruit known as the Apple of Sodom, eyes of sheep, blood and earth — these are all gathered together when ceremonies take place."

The Prosecution sought to prove that Jomo Kenyatta had been associated with Mau Mau even after its proscription in 1950. He himself was described as "an exceptionally widely travelled and educated African who has had the advantage of contact with a great many people of standing both in Kenya and in Europe . . . Perhaps the shortest and best description of Jomo Kenyatta is that he is in a class by himself." The Prosecutor then said he would prove that Mau Mau was a "militant part" of K.A.U., and he compared it with the Jewish terrorist organization called the Stern Gang, which had caused the British a good deal of trouble in Palestine after the war.

And so the trial got under way. It was five months and nearly a million words later before it ended, and another fifteen months before appeals and a petition had been dealt with. The course of this trial, with its moments of drama, humour, boredom, and anger, is well described by Montagu Slater in his book, *The Trial of Jomo Kenyatta*. Kenyatta himself of course denied the accusation levelled against him. Sometimes he became aroused and made long speeches on the wrongs that had been suffered by the Kikuyu. Sometimes he obviously enjoyed using his wit at the expense of the Prosecution, as when, after being questioned about his travels in Europe, he listed a string of countries, ending, after a deliberate pause, with Russia. Towards the end of the long proceedings he appeared to be getting tired, and sometimes stammered and lost the thread of his thoughts.

There is a widespread belief among Africans in Kenya that the trial was "rigged" by the Government. As far as procedure is concerned, however, it was as accurate as most trials, and meticulous attention was paid to almost ludicrous details, such as the ownership of an informer's coat, or the thickness of a door through which a police informer claimed to have heard a Mau Mau ceremony. The Prosecution picked its way through the tangle of lies, half-truths, and doubts with some skill. The Defence, with equal skill, uncovered contradictions and tripped up incompetent police informers. There were heated arguments about the exact meaning of various Kikuyu words. Shortly before his arrest Kenyatta had made a speech in which he had used a Kikuyu curse on Mau Mau, which in English meant that Mau Mau was to disappear down into the roots of a particular type of tree. The Prosecution, which took the Government line that whenever Kenyatta had denounced Mau Mau he and his audience both knew that he had not meant what he said, said that this curse was a cunning way of indicating that Mau Mau should go underground. I have asked many Kikuyu about this point and all have insisted that Kenyatta meant what he appeared to mean.

Whatever the truth of this, it is clear that there was a laborious attempt to examine all possible details. One man, who claimed to have been a friend of Kenyatta's and to have drunk himself "silly" with him on several occasions, said that in 1950 he had heard singing going on all night at Kenyatta's house and that in the morning he had seen people with cuts on their wrists and thought that they had been initiated into Mau Mau. Defence wondered why he had waited two years to tell the police, said that his house was out of earshot of Kenyatta's home, and suggested that he had made up the whole story. Witnesses were called to deny the story. A District Commissioner told the court how Kenyatta had been evasive about denouncing Mau Mau, but agreed when Pritt suggested that it was unwise for a political leader to spend his time denouncing things rather than advocating his own policies.

One of the accused, Paul Ngei, was said to have written from Nairobi prison to a friend saying that he amused himself singing his own version of a song made popular in England by George Formby, called "Bless 'Em All," and that his own words were "Bless Mau Mau." Defence maintained that there was a South African European prisoner in a nearby cell who sang these words facetiously and that the accused merely copied him. Apart from such apparent trivialities there was difficulty in drawing a line between legitimate Kikuyu ceremonies and those of Mau Mau. One question and answer from the Prosecutor to a Kikuyu-speaking police officer will serve to demonstrate this obstacle to truth.

The Prosecutor: ". . . the eyes were taken out of the head, that is, the goat's head, and these eyes were placed on the side of the calabash and were stuck on thorns. Has that got any significance of any society or body of men?"

Police Officer: "Yes, it is significant in the Mau Mau and it is also — the eyes of goats; sheep are also used in ordinary Kikuyu ceremonies relating to land."

A prosecution witness said that Kenyatta had administered one of the milder Mau Mau oaths to him in 1950, but under cross-examination he admitted that in an earlier statement made to the police he had not mentioned Kenyatta but someone else as the oath administrator.

And so it went on. Under cross-examination Kenyatta

gave a spirited defence of his political aims. He denied that
he was anti-English and said that what he hated was the
new form of slavery which had been imposed on the Africans. "While formerly a man could walk and feel like a
man," he told the Prosecutor, "we were subjected to the
humiliation of the colour bar and everything." In response
to a list of grievances the Prosecutor interrupted sarcasti-
cally, "That must be terrible. Yes, go on." "Well, it is terrible.
If I were to change with you, sir, and you be an African,
occupy an African position, and I occupy your position, I
bet you will not stay one week or even two days in the
African position. You do not know it, and you think he is
happy, but he is not happy."

He described as "utter nonsense" a suggestion that he
had planned to drive Europeans out of Kenya. "You people
have audacity to ask me silly questions," he said, "I have
done my best and if all other people had done as I have
done, Mau Mau would not be as it is now. You made it
what it is, not Kenyatta." Then came the final speech for
the Crown, and among other things the Prosecutor said
that Kenyatta tried to impress the Court as a "curious cross
between, say, Gandhi and a boy scout," although he seemed
to contradict this somewhat, later on, by describing his
mind as filled with "great bitterness." He took the line
shared by the Government, that Kenyatta had deliberately
created Mau Mau for his own ends. The Magistrate, as we
have seen, agreed.

In his judgment the Magistrate said he did not think
Kenyatta was a truthful witness, but "all the Prosecution
witnesses impressed me as speaking the truth." He noted
the strong objection by all the accused to the colour bar
and said, "I feel some of the underlying causes for their
actions is their obsession about what is called the colour bar

or alleged racial discrimination." He thought that all the accused had "taken advantage of the uneducated and primitive Africans in order to further their own ambitious purposes and their lust for power."

In a short speech on behalf of himself and the other accused, Kenyatta repeated what he had said so often in the past years of his life: that all that he and the others wanted was that Africans should be treated as human beings with their own rights.

". . . We feel that this case, from our point of view, has been so arranged as to make scapegoats of us in order to strangle the Kenya African Union, the only African political organization which fights for the rights of the African people. We wish to say that what we have done in our activities has been to try our level best to find ways and means by which the community in this country can live in harmony. But what we have objected to — and we shall continue to object — are the discriminations in the government of this country. We shall not accept that, whether we are in gaol or out of it, sir, because we find that this world has been made for human beings to live in happily . . . What we have done, and what we shall continue to do, is to demand the rights of the African people as human beings . . . We look forward to the day when peace shall come to this land and that the truth shall be known that we, as African leaders, have stood for peace. None of us would be happy or would condone the mutilation of human beings. We are humans and we have families . . . we stand for the rights of the African people, that Africans may find a place among the nations."

By contrast was the Magistrate, passing sentence: ". . . When they have made so much progress towards an enlightened civilization, you have successfully plunged many of them back to a state which shows little of humanity . . . You have let loose upon this land a flood of misery and unhappiness affecting the daily lives of all the races in it, including your own people. You have put the clock back many years and by your deeds much of the respect for your tribe has been lost, at least for the time being." Each of the accused was sentenced to seven years' hard labour, to be followed by indefinite restriction.

So, after five weary months the "Queen," alias the Kenya Government, had won the next round against Jomo Kenyatta, the African who, after fifty years of British settlement and colonization, was so far ahead of his fellows in ability that he had been officially described as being in a "class by himself." Even assuming that the verdict was just in every respect, it was a poor reflection on the "civilizing mission" that its most highly educated product had been found guilty of promoting an insane move to kill every European in Kenya. But was he guilty?

Even in the narrow sense of active complicity in Mau Mau, was Kenyatta, on the evidence provided by the Crown, manager of a society which, on the admission of the Crown, had no records and no members? From a strictly legal point of view, opinion in Kenya is divided. One of the star prosecution witnesses was later found guilty of perjury, and was described by a man who knew him well as a "pathological liar." Of the two men who actually claimed to have seen Kenyatta administering a Mau Mau oath one had previously made a statement to the police about the same event in which Kenyatta's name never appeared, and the other could have had ulterior motives for his denunciation. This, and the thin evidence of police informers, allied with the fact that Kenyatta had enormous influence with the Kikuyu people and was therefore felt to have been able to stop Mau Mau had he wished to do so, seems to have been the main basis for conviction.

But even if the evidence of the prosecution witnesses is believed, there is still no proof that Kenyatta had any part in the formulation of the really degrading aspects of Mau Mau, which were first noted just before his arrest, and which degenerated still further later on. The Kikuyu traditionally used oaths to promote unity in times of stress. In those far-off days in 1922 when Harry Thuku and the "mission boys" were first trying their strength against the Government, there had been oaths in enforcing unity. But in those days the oath had shown signs of evolving into something entirely unobjectionable. The Bible was used by the participants. Later, as frustration grew in face of a rigidly unimaginative Government, the oath mystique cut itself off from any links with the new civilization, and the psychological retreat began. It is possible that at this stage Jomo Kenyatta decided to try to use the dangerous energies of the growing numbers of embittered young men in Nairobi. Words had so conspicuously failed to influence Government policy that he might have felt that a certain amount of violence might do it. As can be seen from the early Mau Mau oaths, they were no more and no less "wicked" than the ideas which motivated the EOKA gunmen, who claimed Archbishop Makarios as a leader; or the Jewish gunmen who fought to create Israel; or the Phoenix Park gunmen in Ireland; or even those thousands of young Indians who, but for the extraordinary influence of Gandhi and the last-minute wisdom of the British, nearly attacked their British rulers in Nehru's name.

It is more than a mere historical coincidence that the

Irish rebellion offers a close parallel with Mau Mau. Land was the focus of nationalism there too, and in 1881 there were 4,439 agrarian outrages committed. Gladstone, a magnificent exponent of the suitable "moral attitude," said of Parnell's Land League: "with fatal and painful precision the steps of crime dogged the steps of the Land League." His comment on Parnell foreshadows the Magistrate's comment on Kenyatta: he "stood between the living and the dead, not like Aaron to stay the plague but to spread the plague."

But Mau Mau differed from its precedents in one important respect. It lacked almost completely, by the time it had burst out in full flood in 1952, that small element of free will and conscious decision which serves as a regenerative spark in most other outbreaks of that emotional storm called nationalism. In fact it proved so serious a disease that it came near to killing the Kikuyu spirit irretrievably, as had happened to many Red Indian tribes and other peoples who have been so demoralized by an alien culture that they have not even had the will to fight back. For those thousands of men who formed the so-called "hard core" of Mau Mau, after the arrest of their idol, Kenyatta, almost the last link with any kind of sanity was snapped. To all intents and purposes these men became lunatics.

The case of Dedan Kimathi, who became the main leader of the Mau Mau forest gangs, shows the abject state of mind which had developed. Born illegitimate, he had a stormy childhood, then later became an habitual liar, a clever thief, a dreamer of dreams about his destiny, and a social castoff. He would have been a difficult member of any society. In Kenya he became a criminal lunatic, calling himself, amongst other things, the "King of Africa,"

"Sir Dedan Kimathi," and the "Popular Prime Minister of the Southern Hemisphere." For three years he exerted an hypnotic influence over his less powerful followers, and developed, as well as an incredibly skilful forest-craft, an endless repertoire of sadistic brutality. The story of this man, typical of thousands of others, though more colourful, will serve as a sad monument to the spine-chilling complacency of British rule in Kenya.

The Magistrate may have won a brief victory for the Queen at Kapenguria, but history will reveal its irony. In fact the British Government did nothing but succeed in convicting itself. Even more than Kenyatta, Mau Mau was the inexorable product of a seriously distorted social system — the product of one of those myths which make nonsense of an age of "scientific humanism."

Evidence of the blind compulsive nature of Mau Mau can be seen in the pathetic military record of the terrorists. In four years of bitter fighting only thirty-two European civilians were killed, and sixty-three members of the security forces. By contrast, 11,503 Mau Mau were killed by soldiers and police, and hundreds more hanged. Nearly two thousand Africans were killed by Mau Mau. Not one train was derailed in all this time, and ambushes were few and usually badly organized. Like lunacy itself, Mau Mau had no records and no members, and almost no direction.

While the trial was dragging on at Kapenguria, Kenya assumed more and more the appearance of civil war. There seemed to be almost an air of relief among some settlers that unbearable psychological tensions could now be relieved by direct action. During one of his continental tours the American writer John Gunther visited Kenya at the height of the emergency and recorded his impressions. "At our first dinner-party in Nairobi," he wrote (later the experience became commonplace), "I discovered that ladies of gentle breeding, in diaphanous evening dress, carried revolvers in their gold-mesh bags, which clanked ominously when they were dropped casually on coffee tables. A youth who looked as if he had just come off a cricket field said with cold, sinister pride that he had shot and killed five Africans so far, and hoped that there would be more to come."[2] Another visitor to Nairobi during Mau Mau was Richard Crossman, one of the more independent spirits in the British Labour party. "Mau Mau," he said afterwards, "is only the first of these compulsive African protests. The fact that its obscenities have so far been met only by brutal and completely uncomprehending repression has intensified the racial hatred which is tearing Kenya apart. In South Africa the White Herrenvolk is big enough to hold its own in a race war for many years. In Kenya, and indeed in all East Africa, it can only save itself from extinction by abdicating its privileges while there is still time. But that means giving up the dream of White ascendancy; and though there are stirrings of conscience in Nairobi, I met no one who seriously contemplated doing that."[3] The military commander brought out from England to deal with Mau Mau, an ebullient Scotsman called General Sir George Erskine, admitted "there is no military answer to Mau Mau; it is purely a political problem of how Europeans, Africans, and Asians can live in harmony."[4]

In the Kikuyu Reserve, the inevitable consequences of using force to deal with a political question became quickly apparent. Nearly half of the 200,000 Kikuyu "squatters"

[2] *Inside Africa,* John Gunther, p. 305.

[3] *New Statesman,* Jan. 23, 1956.

[4] Quoted in an article by Colin Legum in *"London Calling,"* May 6, 1954.

living on European farms were either sacked or left of their own accord, and drifted back into the already drastically overcrowded Reserve. Unemployed and hungry, they became willing recruits for the forest gangs, who had been driven out of the villages into the hills by the soldiers. Collective fines, curfews, and severe restrictions on movement were used to smother the rebellion. Unable to speak the language, and totally ignorant of the political and social issues at stake, soldiers and police tended to regard every African they saw as a member of Mau Mau. The latent fear in the European mind that the cherished myth of white supremacy might be false began to claim human sacrifices. A man who managed to escape from the carnage swore to me that he and two dozen other Mau Mau suspects were put in a lorry and driven to the edge of the forest, when they were told to get out and disappear. As they ran into the trees, he said, they were shot down by Bren-gun fire. There were too many stories of this kind for them all to be false. One British officer was sentenced to five years' imprisonment for "disgraceful conduct." From the journal of the Devonshire Regiment a British M.P. quoted, "As 'D' Company claimed a Mau Mau on the same day the Commanding Officer's prize of £5 for the first kill had to be shared." "C" Company was also lucky. In one area "the lack of Mau Mau was to a certain extent compensated for by an abundance of elephant, rhinoceros, baboons and all types of buck . . ." and as a whole "our record up to date, of which we are justly proud, reads twenty-four killed, four captured."

More and more people in Britain became disturbed by the flood of atrocity stories which started to come in. The myth had begun to disintegrate on the hard facts of experience. In 1954, while Kenyatta was still in the remote prison at Lokitaung, a parliamentary delegation visited Kenya. England was about to try to extricate herself once more from a tight corner. In a House of Commons debate on the colour bar the Liberal leader, Joseph Grimond, ridiculed the perennial racialist fear of intermarriage by saying he did not mind if his daughter married a black man provided he was kind to his father-in-law. The Union Debating Society at Cambridge University passed a motion which read: "The White Man's Burden has rested too long on black shoulders."

However, even in 1954 the parliamentary delegation was able to report of Nairobi: "Mau Mau orders are carried out in the heart of the city. Mau Mau 'courts' sit in judgment and their sentences are carried out by gangsters." Soon afterwards, more than 25,000 Kikuyu were rounded up in Nairobi and sent to "screening" camps. The Director of Operations in Kenya said on June 7, 1954: "What every soldier wanted was a kind of 'swill-tub' in a large area where 100,000 Kikuyu could be put out of the way on works projects and told that they were there for life."

But the parliamentary delegation saw beyond a need for "swill-tubs" and, though pointing out that Mau Mau influence was still increasing in the Kikuyu Reserve, and even outside, it ended its political recommendations on a radical note. "We believe," it said, ". . . that it is necessary to provide an outlet for African political thought . . . Africans should be encouraged to develop their own political organisations, thus filling the vacuum created by the banning of the Kenya African Union for complicity in Mau Mau." It had required the catastrophe of Mau Mau to awaken realistic liberalism in British colonial politics.

But this only marked the opening round in the battle to establish a Government based on hard facts and not myth. The next few years were to see some startling changes. By 1956, at a cost of thousands of lives, more than 50 million pounds, and an untold amount of human misery, Mau Mau was reduced to a handful of terrorists lurking in the hills and forests. In March 1957 what was known as the Lyttelton Plan was put into effect. At last Africans were allowed to vote, although on a restricted franchise, and eight Africans were elected. One African was made a Minister.

But what might have been manna from heaven in 1951 was now regarded as little less than an insult. The African members, elected by what the Government naïvely hoped were "moderates," immediately boycotted this constitution on the grounds that they had never agreed to it. They demanded another fifteen seats, which would have given them a majority over all other elected members. In 1958 the Lennox-Boyd constitution was introduced, giving the Africans six more elected members. With reluctance the Africans agreed to this, but showed their displeasure by walking out of the Legislative Council during the Governor's reading of the Queen's speech. This constitution tottered for one year, but by the end of 1959 African pressure had again won a victory and the Colonial Secretary, Mr. Macleod, came out to Kenya to see what was happening.

After a short hard look at the political scene he summoned a conference of elected members in London. Early in 1960 the Macleod constitution was hammered out. In the face of strong opposition from most of the settlers, but with the support of a small number of the more liberal among them, the Africans were for the first time promised a majority of elected members, to be elected early in 1961. In a few quick years the myth of white supremacy had

collapsed like a pricked balloon, but there was quite a mess
to clear up.

Economic gains almost kept up with the political rush
forward. Africans began to grow coffee in ever larger
quantities, and with a success which made nonsense of the
earlier settler objections. African housing became a major
preoccupation of the Government. African business began
to mushroom all over Kenya, most hotels became accessible
to all races, and racial pay scales began to disappear. Quite
suddenly the African was within easy reach of mastery in
his own home, and the question arose as to what he would
then do with the Europeans and the Indians. What had the
Kenya African himself become since Mau Mau revealed
the full disastrous consequences of Government policy?
His own wants unexplored for so long, would he explore
the wants of those within his control? Would he teach the
"civilizing mission" by example where it went wrong? No
one could answer these questions with any certainty, but
the enigma of Jomo Kenyatta lay at the heart of the matter. He was the man who had done more than anyone to
awaken African political consciousness. Africans from all
tribes had acknowledged this by building him into a symbol of African unity and strength, and by loudly demanding his release. But Kenya Europeans, with a few exceptions, were determined to fly their discredited balloon to
the last breath of air.

Once again they were in danger of achieving disaster.
They persisted in making Jomo Kenyatta the whipping boy
of their fears, although they knew very well that he might
soon be able to rule them. They might shake their heads
dejectedly over the pace of events in the past few years,
and blame America, or Mr. Macleod, or "wishy-washy"
liberals in England, but to let Kenyatta return to political

life would be to admit that they had spent most of their political life in a world of make-believe, and face not only facts but the risk of revenge. They no longer had the certainty that they were right, but could they find a way of escaping the past, and its possible consequences? Somehow they had to face the meaning of their myth, and they could do this only by facing the implications of Jomo Kenyatta's life, and his influence over the Africans.

CHAPTER ELEVEN

THE MAN AND THE MYTH

DURING HIS seven years in the small desert prison of Lokitaung, Kenyatta was cut off from any direct political contact, although he doubtless heard rumours of what was happening in the outside world. After six hectic years of intense political strain there must have been at least an element of relief in the endless and trivial routine which now enveloped his life. In fact he later told a lawyer who visited him that his "enforced rest" had not been without its uses. Particularly during his later restriction at Lodwar, after he had served his prison sentence, he had access to books and papers.

On account of his age and physical condition he did not do any of the "hard labour" to which he had been sentenced, and instead, on behalf of the prisoners, practised the skill at cooking which he had found so useful in wartime England. Nerves quickly frayed during these hot and purposeless years, and sometimes there were fights among the prisoners, in the course of which Kenyatta's reading glasses were broken at least three times. Suddenly cut off from his tribe, politics, the life of an awakening African Kenya, and confined to this remote human cage, Kenyatta's strong vitality reached a low point.

In 1959 he was moved to another far-off outpost called Lodwar, where he still remained at the end of 1960. At Lodwar he has lived under what is officially called "restriction," which means that he can move about the village, and has the use of a small Government cottage as a home. He also has a small area of land, but it is said that he has shown little interest in it. Perhaps, after the lush soil of Kikuyuland, he finds making the desert bloom a thankless task. The heat is oppressive throughout the year, and he often complains of it in his letters to friends and relatives. Letters are carefully censored by a Government official in Nairobi, but he receives newspapers and listens to the radio. Visitors are few and far between, and have been confined to close relatives, a lawyer or two, and occasional Government officials. Kenyatta has rigidly refused to have any kind of formal contact with the Government, and in August 1960 he treated a visiting party of Ministers with great coolness. As the Minister for Information told me with a sigh, "He regards himself as the government-in-exile." Kenyatta has a monthly allowance from the Government of 9 pounds.[1]

But what, meanwhile, has happened to his mind? Under the pressures of prison life a man with the dynamic personality of Jomo Kenyatta must change, or go mad. The other alternatives are philosophical resignation or an increasingly hopeless bitterness. There is evidence that Kenyatta has moved towards the former, although his interest in Kenya's political development remains very strong. A Government official who saw him in 1959 told me that Kenyatta had in his cottage a good collection of works on comparative religion, and added, "He is the first African I have met with a deep appreciation of Western classical music."

There is other evidence that Kenyatta has been taking a deep interest in finding a religious belief which matches

[1] Written Autumn 1960.

his experience. This is not at all surprising as from his first years he has shown how naturally his mind turns to religious matters, first within the traditional Kikuyu mould, and then towards a synthesis of the many conflicting examples of Christianity as an "undenominational" Christian. Like many thinking Africans, Kenyatta quickly found the various European manifestations of Christianity too restricted and exclusive for his needs. Hence, perhaps, the impression of somewhat cynical detachment which orthodox churchmen in Kenya sometimes claim to have remarked in his attitude to their faiths.

His old friend from his time in England, Dinah Stock, now a teacher in India, told me that soon after going to prison Jomo Kenyatta wrote to her and asked for a number of books. These included works on Hinduism, Buddhism, and Confucianism, and he told her that he wanted to make a serious study of oriental religions. He wanted, he said, to trace the origin of the philosophy of nonviolence in Hindu thought. In subsequent letters he said he found difficulty in finding this source, but had been particularly impressed with the Bhagavad-Gita.

A fiery little Indian bookbinder in Nairobi, who is an almost fanatical supporter of Kenyatta, and would die a hundred times for him if he had half a chance, told me that Kenyatta had asked for a copy of the *Gita Rahashya*, a book written in a Burmese prison in 1905 by B. G. Tilak, one of the initiators of Indian nationalism. Mr. Ambu Patel, himself a veteran of India's struggle for independence, told me that not long ago he had also been asked by Kenyatta to bind for him a series of articles on man's evolution which had appeared in a well-known American magazine. Jomo Kenyatta has been so impressed by his new studies, apparently, that he recently told one of the lawyers who had defended him at Kapenguria that he almost felt himself to be a Hindu. Perhaps he may later try to give Africans in Kenya a lead in finding a way through the jungle of conflicting beliefs which bedevil any attempt to forge a spiritual base for nationalist politics.

Prison and restriction do not seem to have altered Kenyatta's easy charm of manner. A European doctor who saw quite a lot of him in 1959 said, "He is a man with the most striking personality, and much charm. You have to keep reminding yourself of what he did to stop liking him." Although he gets depressed by the heat he remains quite cheerful and, given an opportunity, he will launch into a political speech. While discussing certain aspects of an impending libel case with his lawyer recently, he frequently tried to state his political convictions, much to the embarrassment of the lawyer, who had been granted the interview on condition that politics were taboo.

Politics, however, cannot be silenced in Kenya, as the young Winston Churchill recognized a long time ago. From the barren site of his "government-in-exile," Kenyatta's influence on Kenya's politics has been dominant. Few of his pronouncements have filtered through to the forums of Nairobi from this dusty Olympus, but his silence is equally potent. He has said that he has been so hit by the colour bar in the past that he will never use discrimination as a counter-weapon. He has warned against the dangers of drink, as he did many years before. He has appealed for African unity, and has said that he is keenly interested in political development. He is said to have given his support to the stronger African political group, composed mainly of Kikuyu and Luo tribes, and which includes such influential men as Dr. Kiano and the forceful Tom Mboya. But the other African group denies this and also claims him as its leader. In late 1960, therefore, after an eight-year absence from the political scene, and despite a nonstop barrage of condemnation from both the Kenya Government and a large part of the world press, it was true to say that Kenyatta exerted more political influence than he ever did before his trial.

In the days when political consciousness in Kenya was confined mainly to the Kikuyu tribe and those Africans working in Nairobi, few of the other tribes knew much about him. The shock of Mau Mau, events in other parts of Africa, and education have all helped to alter that. In a search for leadership which transcends tribal loyalty, and which has enough vision to unite the many confusing elements in modern African life, Africans in Kenya turned almost unanimously to Jomo Kenyatta. This allegiance to a man in exile was denounced by some Europeans as an "escape into symbolism" and a search for a "father-figure." It may have been both these things, but it also had a good deal of solid evidence to support its practical validity. Most Africans in Kenya knew very well that what Kenyatta asked for in the years after the war was due to them as human beings. They did not believe that he was responsible for the outrages of Mau Mau, but they knew that after Mau Mau political development shot forward. If this was just a coincidence then it was a very odd one.

Whether or not it is agreed that there were good reasons for this choice of leadership, it remained a political fact of the first importance. By 1960, what Africans wanted had begun to matter a very great deal politically. The exploration of African wants had begun, for the first time in Kenya's history as a British colony, to take place on a wide scale. There were elected African Ministers, there was an attempt to speed the "Africanisation" of business and the

Civil Service, and only a few shabby smudges of the colour bar were left on the new canvas. An Act of Grace by the Governor permitted the return to normal life of many Mau Mau detainees. But over the question of Kenyatta a stalemate had been reached.

After the provisions of the 1960 Macleod constitution had been announced, the campaign to "free Kenyatta" began to warm up. Country-wide petitions were signed, letters were written to the papers, speeches were made. But the new Governor, Sir Patrick Renison, a genial man with a fatherly manner, acted on the advice of his senior officials and announced, on March 31, 1960, that "the release of Jomo Kenyatta would be a danger to security." It was officially feared that Kenyatta's return would raise the political temperature to a dangerous level, and that those Kikuyu who had fought with the Government against Mau Mau would be persecuted by their former enemies. There was an element of truth in this, but no more. Many so-called "Kikuyu Loyalists," whose names have been so shamelessly invoked by many Europeans striving to fend off African control, did no more than join what they thought at the time was the winning side. As Dr. Carothers wrote, referring to the fact that very few Kikuyu identified themselves with the Kenya Government: ". . . loyalty in the full sense of the word is hardly to be looked for at the moment."[2] There were a few Kikuyu who fought Mau Mau for religious reasons, and some were killed for their courage, but there is no proof that there were more than a handful of "Loyalists" who objected to Kenyatta's return for any better reason than they had misused Government support by helping themselves to the property of detainees, and feared revenge. One "Loyalist," a man in a responsible

[2] *Op. cit.*, p. 20.

Government post, told me that by harping on this thread-
bare loyalty the Government was not helping the cause of
unity, but aggravating it.

It seemed as if the real Act of Grace would not be made
— the grace to admit that the Kenya Government, and the
British Government, had committed a terrible misjudg-
ment in causing the growth of Mau Mau by its negligence
of African wants. It was just possible to pretend to the
world that Kenya's belated rush towards independence
was a result of planning instead of an awkward conscience,
combined with strong political pressure; and it was possible to advertise the release of Mau Mau terrorists as a
magnanimous "Act of Grace." But to release Kenyatta
would be to risk a demonstration to the world that the
Kenya Government had been fundamentally wrong in its
estimation of his character and his political aims. If Kenyatta proved to be the sort of leader whom the Africans
believed him to be, then nobody would any longer believe
the official story of his management of Mau Mau. If this
happened, then the Government would have to account
elsewhere for the emergence of Mau Mau, and no lesser
scapegoat than Kenyatta would serve adequately as a
promoter of chaos on such a large scale.

Of course, the Kenya Government did not think pre-
cisely in these Machiavellian terms, for the good reason
that it was barely conscious of its own myth, and within the
terms of the myth it was merely doing its duty. But the
effect of this continued flirtation with fantasy was potentially disastrous to the future stability of Kenya. The Europeans might fool themselves, but they could no longer fool
the Africans, and the Africans knew that they wanted
Kenyatta back to lead them. It seemed as if the Kenya

Government was going to repeat the performance of Gerald Bullett's character:

> *Who blew his brains out on the bedroom floor,*
> *And then behaved exactly as before.*

In face of mounting pressure for the release of Jomo Kenyatta the Governor made a broadcast to the colony in which he solemnly, and with an air of sincere conviction, set out his reasons for keeping Kenyatta where he was. The speech won almost universal approval among Kenya Europeans. Some extracts will give an idea of the depth and importance of this clash with African opinion.

He began by referring to his recent statement that, in the prevailing circumstances, "the release of Jomo Kenyatta would be a danger to security." "Since then," he said, "I have continued to receive memorials and petitions and other representations asking me to release Jomo Kenyatta from restriction . . . The pressures of the campaign for his release are growing. I therefore wish to state at some length the reasons for my recent decision and for its information.

"During the Kenya debate in the House of Lords on the 28th March, 1960, the Lord Archbishop of Canterbury twice referred to the African struggle between light and darkness, life and death. I believe that there is such a struggle and that here in Kenya Africans are at the crisis of that struggle." The Governor then went on to refer to the latent tendency to violence in African, and particularly in Kikuyu, politics. "The culmination of such non-co-operation and violence," he went on, "was the struggle for Kikuyu domination known as the Mau Mau movement, a rebellion of fearful oaths and fearful deeds, whose terror-ism, savagery and bestiality shocked the world. It tore the African peoples of Kenya asunder and it cast doubts on the ability of African leaders in Kenya to separate politics from violence and intimidation."

Sir Patrick then said that Jomo Kenyatta had been convicted by the due processes of law as the leader of Mau Mau. "Here," he said, "was the African leader to darkness and death," and continued gravely: "It has taken years to put the horrors of Mau Mau behind us. Anyone who seeks to resurrect its antagonisms or its intimidations and violence is an enemy of Kenya, a confederate of the old terrorist Africa of darkness and death. The unenlightened days of violent opposition to the Government should now be past. I pray God that the divisions of the Kikuyu peoples and of African politics generally may end."

Sir Patrick added that the new constitution ensured that independence would come soon and that Africans would have the dominant say in it. "The way is clear," he said, "to light and life in a modern world, as opposed to darkness and death in a throw-back world that is past. It is the responsibility of those Africans who are not blind to it to convince their people." He added that he wished to help Kenya show the world that the time of "darkness" was past and that every community in the colony would play its part.

He continued: "I have at present no evidence whatsoever that Jomo Kenyatta will help Kenya in these aims. I have much evidence to the contrary. With the assistance of the researches carried out by Mr. D. F. Corfield, I have very carefully studied his life and modes of thought and speech and action, particularly in the period between his return to Kenya in 1946 and the declaration of the emergency in 1952. As I have said, he planned for Kikuyu domination; he was an implacable opponent of any co-operation with other people, tribes or faces, who live in Kenya."

The Governor then made the somewhat strange observation that his decision regarding Kenyatta's release was entirely to do with security and not politics. He thought his return would encourage those who had fought against Government. "The administration," he added, "would be demoralised. His return would tend to glorify Mau Mau and to identify it with African national advance, when the emphasis should be on how much Mau Mau and Jomo Kenyatta's leadership retarded that advance." He repeated that Kenyatta's return would impede constitutional advance by encouraging violence.

"However many people there may be," he went on, "whose marks or signatures or names have been put on bits of paper asking for his release, I must trust my own judgment of what is best for Kenya at this moment of its history . . . I have no hesitation in confirming the decision which I published on 31st March, 1960." He added that the case of every person restricted came up for review at regular intervals and that it was the policy of the Government to return them all to normal life, "however long it takes."

The Governor then concluded his talk: "I ask those who have been leading the campaign for Jomo Kenyatta's release to ponder deeply what I have said about light and darkness and about what we are trying to do for the Africans and the other peoples of this country. The campaign is inflaming old antagonisms and thereby increasing the security reasons for continued restriction. If they wish to hasten his release, the door is not shut. There is one clear way for them. I ask them to work actively, as many leaders are now doing, to bring to an end the divisions and per-

sonal fears among the Kikuyu peoples and other people in
Kenya and to produce an atmosphere of stable political
achievement . . . where the threat of violence and intimidation is no longer a weapon of political or labour movements, and where the old Mau Mau antagonists have entirely disappeared. When such an atmosphere in Kenya is
sufficiently firmly established and has become the pattern,
there will no longer be security danger in the return of
persons who held back Kenya's advance by trying to follow
policies of violence in the past."

Even among those Africans who disagreed entirely with
this speech, and few did not, none doubted the Governor's
personal sincerity. This merely served to make its contents
doubly tragic. Like the clouds which so often blur the
white peaks of Kere-Nyaga, the terrible old myth, which
for so long had obscured the true face of Kenya, still lived
on to distort and darken its politics. To those who knew
that the face of Africa is so easily a smiling face, the Governor's words were a grim reminder of the urgent need to
prevent its being darkened once more unnecessarily. The
"civilizing mission," which had set out with so much
panache at the turn of the century, had become as sadly
irrelevant as the daydreams of a tired old man.

In nearly every respect the Governor's speech missed
political reality. Many, perhaps all, people have myths of
one sort or another which colour their lives. Many can
harm only the possessor, if anyone at all, and few children
suffer from believing in Father Christmas. It can even be
cruel to destroy personal myths maliciously. But when
whole nations or civilizations cherish a myth it can lead to
war and misery, as all make-believe breaks up on reality
in the end. When he made this speech about Jomo Kenyatta, the one and only African leader in Kenya who had

the capacity to bring about unity, the Governor was merely projecting a way of thinking which emanated from Britain herself.

Sir Patrick quoted the Archbishop of Canterbury's reference to the African struggle between "light and darkness, life and death," and then said that Jomo Kenyatta was the leader to "darkness and death." This sad nonsense could only be explained in terms of an England and a modern world which were faced with such almost intolerable problems of spiritual and political reality that they had to look away for comfort. Africa, with its still surviving dependence on Western knowledge, had become the victim of this attempted transfer of responsibility. Slowly but surely Europe had come to need Africa's dependence as a prop to her own wavering self-confidence. By contrast with the "terrorist Africa of darkness and death" of her imagination, Europe's own morality, horribly broken in two catastrophic wars, had assumed an illusory but comforting glow of righteousness.

By expecting "darkness and death" in Africa, a land where the human spirit had grown slowly, but with a balance of its own which had its measure of laughter as well as tears, Europe began to create what it looked for. By offering the fruits of "civilization" with one hand, and taking them away with the other, a state of psychological confusion was caused which became an even more intolerable strain on the African mind. Europe wanted to give, but it was too afraid of itself to give generously. Nationalism grew up, not merely as a natural development, but as a violent revolt against what became a tyranny of good intentions, sometimes vicious in its effects.

Mau Mau, with its violation of the traditional and its pathetic distortion of the modern, was the horrible culmination of a long period of weak government, during which the almost blind trust of the African was stupidly exploited. Jomo Kenyatta never had a real chance to lead his people either to "darkness" or to "light." His remarkable and valuable gifts never had a chance to serve or to mislead, except in the narrowest sense. Soon after his return to Kenya his powers of leadership were relentlessly squeezed into the patterns of a colony held in the compulsive grip of a fantasy. The fantasy was well disguised by lofty phrases about "duty" and "trust." Sir Philip Mitchell was a highly intelligent Governor and something of a philosopher, but his liberal convictions could no more fight their way through the surrounding fantasy than could those of the Labour Government in Britain. Kenya became an expressive testimony to the truth of the saying that without vision a people perish.

Sir Patrick's comments did not include even a hint that the Kenya Government, which was supposed to be in control of Kenya at the time, shared any responsibility for Mau Mau. "I pray God," he said, "that the divisions of the Kikuyu peoples and of African politics generally, may end." And yet, if the wishes of the African people were anything to go by, the only leader they all wanted was the very man he would not let them have. Once more the old compulsive patterns of "preach the truth but make sure it can't happen" were beginning to reappear.

The problems of the Kikuyu peasant tilling his small patch of ground in the clear light of the African sun may have been large, but they were nothing compared with the problems of the Noble Lords in London, balanced as they officially were on a knife-edge of terror. If the Kikuyu peasant had not grown tired of being looked after by people he no longer trusted he might have felt flattered that wise men beyond the seas spared time in their extremity to wag their heads over his fate.

The Governor claimed that Kenyatta "planned for Kikuyu domination," and was an "implacable opponent of any co-operation with other people . . ." If this was true, why did every African political leader in Kenya come to accept him as a leader? The Governor said that if Kenyatta returned "the administration would be demoralised," but there were a number of young European administrators in Kenya who privately expressed a hope that Kenyatta would be freed as the only way of uniting the tribes. It would be a poor sort of administration which became demoralised by the return of a popular leader.

The Governor then said that Kenyatta and his alleged leadership of Mau Mau "held back Kenya's advance . . ." But as has been pointed out already, Kenya's political advance doubled its speed after Mau Mau, and "psychological chaos" was already endemic among the Kikuyu and other Africans when Kenyatta returned from Europe in 1946. The Governor's appeal for an end to disunity among the tribes was like telling a man to play football without allowing him a ball. The African mind in Kenya desperately needed unity, but it knew very well where to find it, if it were allowed to find it.

Once more the tensions between two apparently irreconcilable forces were rising in Kenya, and the future looked grim, dominated as it was by the prospect of a final aggressive victory of African political will power in the face of an ever more unrepresentative and discredited Government. The lessons of Mau Mau were being squandered by a poverty of political vision, and the tyranny of good intentions still held itself to be ultimately more relevant than African wants.

And so, after more than half a century, modern Kenya
seemed to have arrived at the logical conclusion of its
initial impulse. Almost from the start the ideals of radical
England had come into head-on conflict with local expediency and the spiritually enervating ideologies of modern Europe. In theory the ideals had remained in the lead,
and indeed, right up to the fateful visit of the Labour Colonial Secretary in 1951, there was still a chance that enough
generosity could be mustered to allow the African voice
an effective hearing. Even after Mau Mau the way was
open, not merely for a sudden throw-away of political
power, but for the only thing which could restore confidence between white and black, a courageous admission
of past errors. But Britain, which had just kept her head
above water in the mono-racial colonies, where the problems were smaller, proved at each test in Kenya that she
lacked the full courage of her convictions. There developed
an increasing tendency to distort facts to fit the fiction of
"duty" and "trust" and "moral responsibility." The Governors of Kenya were not the men to break through the
inertia at "home."

The Africans, and Jomo Kenyatta among them, who at
first were astounded at the white man's magic and became
increasingly ready to accept what he said he had come to
give, were soon disconcerted by the contradictions of the
new civilization. "Mission boys" came up against a white
wall of segregation and quickly turned sour, awakening the
simple country people to an ever greater awareness of real
and imaginary wrongs. Such was the depth of their will-
ingness to learn the new ways that, right up to 1960, a
sincere gesture from the Europeans, at first merely of normal recognition but in the latter years of something more
magnanimous, would have restored the balance. But so

far it had not come, and as long as Noble Lords in London spoke from a moral false position about the African struggle between "darkness and death" it could not come. The African in Kenya had to make a place for himself in the modern world, and confronted as he was by complex spiritual, economic, and political problems, he had to search for unity wherever it could be found. To deny him this unity, even if it entailed political autocracy, would be extreme cruelty when what was needed was extreme and impossible generosity. Jomo Kenyatta, the man with a wide experience of both worlds, the new and the old, was one of the very few men with the inherent vision to forge this unity.

The political history of the Kenya in which Jomo Kenyatta grew up and developed as a man is a sorry story of things that might have been but never were. Not one leader had been able to control the strong crosscurrent of conflicting interests and make one united stream, but of course, within the inadequate political pattern, as always, human nature made the best of things. Jomo Kenyatta himself, although he was never in a position to do more than push here and there at the course of events, has sustained more of the stresses of these years than any other man. He had a deep conviction in the worth of his own tribe and people, and maintained this faith in face of continued political and moral pressure, although there came a time when he nearly cracked under the strain. He also absorbed European ideas with alacrity, and had the way been open for him, Kenya might have moved into the 1960s in a state of confidence rather than fear, and with an African population which had a genuine confidence in itself.

The British Government, as the principal sponsor of this drama, emerges as a promising character, but with some

fatal weaknesses. Although guardian of a treasure-house of
fine ideals, and initially with great physical power, it had
begun to lose touch with its roots and seldom managed
to keep ahead of events. Under the devastating pressure of
two wars its reserves of liberalism began to dwindle. The
failure of the postwar Labour Government to understand
the problems of Kenya must be held as one of the main
causes of Mau Mau. In later years the British Government
was furtively trying to cover up its past misdeeds, without
much success. In the words of Ewart Grogan, used in
Kenya's Legislative Council to describe an official Minister
whom he suspected of two-way thinking, the British Government emerges from this story more as a "downy old
bird simulating saintliness" than as a dynamic civilizing
agent.

Ewart Grogan himself and many other settlers have sup-
plied an almost endless source of colour in Kenya's life,
with their pungent language and their obstinate individualism. Many have led fine lives in very difficult circumstances, but politically they have failed hopelessly. They
became a highly concentrated and ruthless pressure group,
with many of the same characteristics as the upper middle
class in Victorian England, but in Kenya the working class
was even more vulnerable than it was there. Firm leadership from Britain could have prevented settler politics from
getting out of hand and becoming an adolescent romp with
adult consequences. Lord Delamere will be remembered
less for his pioneering qualities in the days when he used
to sit on the mud floor of his small hut, chat with his Masai
herdsmen and pour the family fortune into agricultural
experiments, than for his futile part in the "Indian Question" and his inability to recognize the facts of Kenya
political life. But it was expecting a lot for a handful of
farmers to rise to the heights of statesmanship which were

demanded of them, and they never received the control from Britain which alone could have curbed them. Britain, if she can find the courage to do so, should take the consequences, whatever they may be, of the political failure of the settlers whom she encouraged to go to Kenya.

Another of the main actors is the missionary, who brought to Kenya all the faults and virtues of religion in Europe. Sometimes narrowly professional and suspicious of rival sects, sometimes arrogant in his approach to traditional African religion, and often unable to impart a faith which could overcome the challenges of a full modern life, he brought to Kenya the religious dilemmas of Europe. With all this he has brought education, medical help, the example of dedicated service, and sometimes a rare spiritual insight and sympathy which has saved some Africans from the psychological chaos which threatened them. But for Kenyatta, and for many of the more educated Africans, missionary influence has been no more helpful than has been the teaching of the churches in Europe for the younger generations.

And what of the "Indian Question," as yet unsettled? Adept at business, gentle of manner, with his graceful women and his subtle religious customs, the Indian has played a valuable part commercially in the life of Kenya. But his future there is uncertain. There is jealousy of his money, there is distaste for his customs, and there is little recognition of his once active support of African rights, often at the expense of anger from the Europeans. Whether he can find a permanent place in Kenya will depend on whether he can emulate the ability of Jewish communities in many countries to merge without loss of their identity. Many leading Indians have given generous support to Kenyatta's political movement.

But it is of course the six million Africans who will decide the future of Kenya. For so long a shadowy and silent figure at the back of the stage, the African has still to feel his full strength. Technically ill-equipped to run a modern society, the African has been left no alternative by the premature breakdown in the morale of his tutor. But he has the dynamic gifts of nationalist energy and natural laughter, and optimism may accomplish miracles. His spontaneous optimism may sweep aside the confusion in his mind, and he may even come to realize that the follies of his rulers have sprung less from wilful malice than the inner torments of Western civilization itself. He may find a new confidence in his own inner resources if he comes to understand that he has for long served Europe both as a mirror and an escape-hatch, as well as an object of benevolence. He may then, when he realizes that it is in Europe and modern civilization that the battle between darkness and death is being fought on a grand scale, even come to sympathize with the plight of the "civilizing mission." It will soon be his problem too.

And this is where Jomo Kenyatta comes in again. At the time of writing it looks as though a reversal of official policy, leading to his release on grounds of "political expediency" early in 1961, may be imminent. When he returns to his people he will have the opportunity, for the first time in his life, of leading Kenya towards a common purpose within the existing realities of the modern world. There is no other African in Kenya who has the experience and the capacity to rise above the potentially explosive confusion which remains on the Kenya stage after sixty-five years of colonial rule. It will be a tragedy of greater dimensions even than Mau Mau if the last twitches of the old myth of white supremacy, or a failure of his own will power under the strain, make this impossible.

BIBLIOGRAPHY

Particulars of Books Mentioned, in Order of First Quotation, for Use in Completing Footnote References

L. S. B. Leakey, *Mau Mau and the Kikuyu* (Methuen), 1952.

Jomo Kenyatta, *Facing Mount Kenya* (Secker and Warburg), 1938.

Ewart S. Grogan and Arthur H. Sharp, *From the Cape to Cairo* (Hurst and Blackett), 1902.

H. K. Binks, *African Rainbow* (Sidgwick and Jackson), 1959.

Winston Spencer Churchill, *My African Journey* (Hodder), 1908.

Karen von Blixen, *Out of Africa* (Random House), 1938.

Sir Charles Eliot, *East African Protectorate* (Arnold), 1905.

Sir Philip Mitchell, *The Agrarian Problem in Kenya* (Nairobi Govt. Press), 1947.

W. McGregor Ross, *Kenya from Within* (Allen R. Unaris), 1927.

Jomo Kenyatta, *Kenya: The Land of Conflict* (Panaf), 1945.

Lord Altrincham, *Kenya's Opportunity* (Faber), 1955.

P. G. Mockerie, *An African Speaks for His People* (Longmans), 1934.

Paul Robeson, *Here I Stand* (Dobson), 1955.

Arthur Koestler, *The Sleepwalkers* (Hutchinson), 1959.

Elspeth Huxley, *A Thing to Love*, (Chatto and Windus), 1954.

Negley Farson, *Last Chance in Africa* (Harcourt), 1950.

Fenner Brockway, *African Journeys* (Gollancz), 1955.

J. C. Carothers, *The Psychology of Mau Mau* (Nairobi Govt. Press), 1954.

Ione Leigh, *In the Shadow of the Mau Mau* (W. H. Allen), 1954.

John Gunther, *Inside Africa* (Harper), 1955.